Gone Dollywood

New Approaches to Appalachian Studies

Series editors: Marie Tedesco and Elizabeth S. D. Engelhardt

Gone Dollywood: Dolly Parton's Mountain Dream, by Graham Hoppe

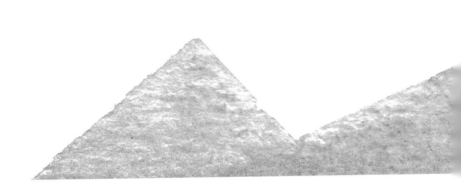

GONE
DOLLYWOOD

Dolly Parton's
Mountain Dream

Graham Hoppe

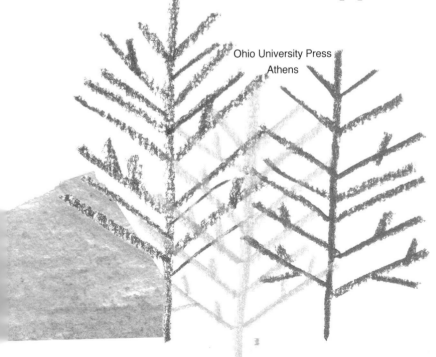

Ohio University Press
Athens

Ohio University Press, Athens, Ohio 45701
ohioswallow.com
© 2018 by Ohio University Press

Jacket and all drawings by Amy S. Hoppe

To obtain permission to quote, reprint, or otherwise reproduce or distribute
material from Ohio University Press publications, please contact our rights
and permissions department at (740) 593-1154 or (740) 593-4536 (fax).

Printed in the United States of America
Ohio University Press books are printed on acid-free paper ⊗ ™

28 27 26 25 24 23 22 21 20 19 18   5 4 3 2 1

Library of Congress Cataloging-in-Publication Data
Names: Hoppe, Graham, 1984- author.
Title: Gone Dollywood : Dolly Parton's mountain dream / by Graham
Hoppe.
Other titles: New approaches to Appalachian studies.
Description: Athens : Ohio University Press, [2018] | Series: New approaches
to Appalachian studies | Includes bibliographical references and index.
Identifiers: LCCN 2017057480| ISBN 9780821423233 (hc : alk. paper) | ISBN
9780821446379 (pdf)
Subjects: LCSH: Dollywood (Pigeon Forge, Tenn.) | Parton, Dolly. | Amusement
parks--Tennessee. | Southern States--Social life and customs.
Classification: LCC GV1853.3.T22 D654 2018 | DDC 791.06/8768893--dc23
LC record available at https://lccn.loc.gov/2017057480

For Amy,
thank you for everything.

And for my parents,
thank you for everything else.

Contents

Illustrations

Acknowledgments

The book you hold in your hand wouldn't exist without the work of Gillian Berchowitz and everyone at Ohio University Press. It is with a deep sense of appreciation that I thank them for providing this work with such a fine home.

This book began as a conversation with William Ferris at the University of North Carolina. It is in no small part thanks to his encouragement and enthusiasm that I began to think of this as a book instead of just an intriguing idea. Bernie Herman, the chair of the American Studies Department at UNC, has provided me with invaluable insight into different ways of thinking about Dollywood. I thank them both for their time and for sharing their incredible depth of knowledge.

With a great sense of gratitude I would like to thank Marcie Cohen Ferris, professor in American Studies at UNC, who has supported and championed this text. Her patience, insight, and editing have made this work possible.

With equal gratitude I would like to thank Elizabeth Engelhardt, coeditor of the Series in Race, Ethnicity, and Gender in Appalachia, who encouraged me to expand an academic piece into this book. These scholars have been an inspiration, and the level of care they have given my work has been an honor.

For joining us at Dollywood for several Christmases, I want to thank my in-laws, David and Debbie Stibich. Last, for reading drafts, providing me with support, and being a constant source of inspiration, I would like to thank my parents, David and Melli Hoppe.

For walking with me every step of the way, from our first visit to Pigeon Forge through my applications to graduate school and the final draft of this book, I thank my wife, Amy Hoppe. I love you, always.

.

Introduction

THIS IS a book about Dollywood.

The natural question that follows is: Why Dollywood? Most people are interested in the place (you probably wouldn't be reading this if you weren't), but I don't think enough people have given the place real thought. They might have thought of it as a kitschy destination or a site for a country music pilgrimage or maybe just a place to ride roller coasters. I think it deserves more. I think it deserves real consideration.

Why should we take Dolly Parton's theme park seriously? First, Dollywood makes a lot of money and keeps a lot of people employed. It is one of a kind—the only theme park dedicated to the persona of a music icon. When I started this project, I knew that its primary focus was going to be an argument about why Dollywood was a serious part of Dolly Parton's deep body of creative work. This book was intended from the beginning to be more like a piece of cultural analysis than a straight history or a biography. If you've come looking for a comprehensive account of Dollywood business deals or insight into rollercoaster construction, I'm afraid I don't have much for you. Likewise, if you're looking for gossip and for Parton's secrets to be revealed, you'll find this volume lacking.

There is history here because history informs Dollywood and Pigeon Forge in ways that are both immediately apparent and more hidden and subtle. There is a bit of politics here too. I know that people don't usually like to be confronted with politics at their vacation destinations, but it can't be helped—we have to talk politics.

I expected a project about Dollywood to revolve almost exclusively around Parton's massive influence, and for the most part that has been the case. However, this story has a few tangential paths that might not be apparent at first glance. The biggest is the Pigeon Forge Parkway, the main thoroughfare of Sevier County's tourist industry. We'll also spend some unexpected time with the celebrity chef Paula Deen, whose restaurant in Pigeon Forge marked the beginning of her comeback from a career-damaging scandal. Speaking of food, there's a stop at Cracker Barrel, the Tennessee-based chain of restaurants that has become a national symbol for what it means to sell the South and for how southern nostalgia can be a complicated and powerful thing.

Despite these detours, the heart of the book is Parton. She sells her own vision of the South, one that speaks to the pride and resilience of Appalachia. I said we won't spend much time dissecting Parton's biography, but we will spend some time with Parton's public persona—the stories she tells in interviews, her autobiography, films, and songs. Parton's persona is such an integral part of her fame and of Dollywood that it is impossible to have any kind of discussion about her without looking at it. She began as the dirt-poor daughter of a sharecropper, a mountain girl who sang songs into a tin can perched on top of a tobacco stick and pretended it was a microphone. She grew into a songwriter and performer who first gained fame as Porter Wagoner's sidekick, but she quickly outgrew the partnership and said good-bye to him with one of the most famous and most successful songs of all time, "I Will Always Love You."

As a solo artist Parton became one of country music's biggest talents, crossing over first into pop music and then into movies with roles in films like *9 to 5* and *Steel Magnolias*. She's won just about every award you can imagine, including a Kennedy Center Honor and the National Medal of Arts.

Along the way Parton has always tried to bend fame in a positive direction. A staunch advocate of education, she founded Dolly Parton's Imagination Library, a literacy charity that has distributed more than sixty million books to children all over the world. Galvanized by her father's illiteracy, Parton understood firsthand how literacy was a key to success. Communities served by the program have consistently shown improved literacy rates and test scores. Parton has also been an advocate for the natural landscape she grew up in. She served as an ambassador for the Great Smoky Mountains National Park during the park's seventy-fifth anniversary celebration. She has also sponsored the American Eagle Foundation, a not-for-profit organization housed at Dollywood that specializes in the rehabilitation and conservation of the bald eagle, a suitably patriotic crowd favorite, and other birds of prey.

These good deeds have further cemented Parton's positive image. She is incredibly popular with a wide range of people. A look at Parton's fans shows that straight, gay, conservative, progressive, evangelical, urban, and rural values are not necessarily incompatible—all are themes in Parton's work.

Oh, and she also has a theme park. It's not just a little vanity tourist trap to mark her place in her hometown—it's the biggest ticketed attraction in the state of Tennessee. More than three million people visit every year. The park features roller coasters and other thrill rides nestled alongside attractions like the Southern Gospel Museum and Hall of Fame, and Chasing Rainbows, a comprehensive museum about Parton's life and career. All told, Parton's amusement empire covers almost three hundred acres in her home county.

What makes Dollywood different? What makes it matter? I think the answer is Parton herself. She is a force of nature who seems relentlessly creative. I've tried hard to keep everything in this book up to date and to use figures and examples that will remain current and relevant throughout the life of this book, but Parton is a moving target. To give you an idea of how difficult it is to keep tabs on her, during the year or so that this book was coming together, Parton announced—and completed—a world tour, unveiled a new roller coaster, purchased a new dinner theater in Pigeon Forge, released two TV movies based on her life and a couple of albums, and began planning a Broadway show. Keeping up with Dolly Parton isn't easy.

I look forward to seeing what she does next. She always seems to be able to surprise. But until then, let's spend some time thinking about what she's already done. I'll see you in the mountains.

Mountains, Parks, and Nothing Less Than Great

I refuse to settle for something less than great.

—Dolly Parton[1]

ROUGHLY AT the center of Dolly Parton's theme park, Dollywood, sits a replica of the two-room cabin where she was born. Both rooms are decorated with ancient-looking furniture and knick-knacks, visible through floor-to-ceiling Plexiglas windows. The viewing area is small, no bigger than a narrow hallway. I stood in that replica in December 2014. It was chilly; the wind whipped the mountain air through wooden walls almost as though they weren't there. Dolly Parton remembers mountain winters in that cabin—the real version. With a sly wink she once told an interviewer that the wind blew snow through the cracks in the wall into straight lines across the floor, "like lines of coke."[2] She's America's naughty girlfriend.

I was alone, comparing the homespun décor with the antiques and knick-knacks I'd seen on the walls of Pigeon Forge's Cracker Barrel, the day before, when a woman in her eighties came into the cabin with her son. They commented on the pages from a Sears and Roebuck catalog that were plastered to the kitchen wall for insulation, feed sack curtains, and *just one bed* for so many people—Dolly has eleven brothers and sisters. Finally, speaking neither to her son nor to me, the woman said, in a voice that sounded like mountains themselves, "It was hard for them. It was hard for us too." The words hung there for a few moments, and then the woman put a hand on her son's arm, looked him in the eyes, and said, "She's never forgotten it, never forgotten us. She's done a lot for her people." The woman's son agreed and they made their way out of the cabin, into the fantastical wonderland that Dolly Parton has presented to her people. I stayed for a few moments more—wanting to feel the woman's words in that space for another instant or two. Then I stepped out of the cabin into the park. The Christmas lights had come on, illuminating the trees around me. It had begun to snow.

~

A few months later I headed to Dollywood again. This visit was near the end of the summer. My wife and I went back to see two things: Dollywood's new resort and Dolly Parton herself. I'd never seen Parton in concert before. Seeing her in her hometown theme park, staying at her newly opened resort, and seeing her perform would be a complete immersion in Parton's empire.

As we drove into town I found myself wondering how Parton managed the logistics of coming home. How she balanced the professional obligations of being the face of a major business—*the* major business—in a tourist town with seeing friends and family. Not to mention getting in and out of town through traffic and to wherever she needed to go without creating too much of scene. Even though she seems like the luxury tour bus type, as we passed Pigeon Forge's tiny municipal airport I wondered whether the airport was built for her. As we passed her alma mater, Sevier County High School, I also wondered if she had ever gone back to see her former teachers.

I had heard that the school has a plaque dedicated to Parton in its hallway. So I called to see if it had any other markers commemorating Parton's time there. The librarian told me that she had forgotten about the plaque and, other than the occasional local who comes in looking for Dolly's yearbook picture, no one makes much fuss about the school's most famous alumna. The librarian told me that the students were mostly aware of Parton's connection to the school through her financial support. Parton's charitable efforts are credited with cutting the dropout rate in Sevier County by half. At one point she offered to pay every student who graduated $500 so long as they could convince a buddy to stay in school as well. Today she awards three $15,000 scholarships a year to the students. "There are quite a few kids who are the first in their family to go to college because of Dolly Parton," the librarian told me.

When Parton came back to her hometown, she used to stay at her theme park. Since the park opened in 1986, Parton had kept a private apartment above one of the park buildings. The apartment was a kind of semi-open secret. The exact location was a mystery, but fans knew it existed and whispered about where exactly it might be. Evidently Parton got tired of being her own theme park's only resident, and in 2010 the space was refurbished as office space for park executives. As a fund-raiser for the local medical center, Parton auctioned off her bedroom furniture—and revealed photos of the suite. The room looks a little like a dollhouse come to life. Everything in it is very pink, very ornate, and a little dated.[3] The bed brought more than four grand on eBay.

When it was announced that Parton was building a new resort, I was curious to know if she had a new apartment built there. I can't quite imagine the logistics of shuttling Dolly Parton through her own lobby and past her fans to her own elevator. It seems logistically almost impossible. I know how intensely some of Parton's fans love her. It's not hyperbolic to say that they worship her.

In a memorable scene in Tai Uhlmann's 2008 documentary, *For the Love of Dolly,* two superfans track down the used car of Parton's assistant and lifelong friend, Judy Ogle, on the lot of Darrell Waltrip's Honda dealership in Franklin, Tennessee.[4] They crawl through the car and pick through the upholstery looking for stray bottle-blonde strands of hair. "This one has a root!" one exclaims. The real coup, though, is when they rummage through the glove box and find an old insurance card issued to both Ogle and Parton. Like ecstatic Pentecostals they lay hands on the passenger seat, where they figure Dolly's rear spent most of its time in the car.

As we drive toward Dolly's resort, I think about that scene. Actually, when I think about Parton, I think about that scene a lot. There's something unnerving about that kind of devotion. To know the make and model of Judy Ogle's car seems to represent a profound level of personal knowledge about Parton's life. The superfans profiled in the film aren't shown to present any particular threat, but it is still a little uncomfortable to see. Imagine what it would be like to mean so much to so many people. That is celebrity on its most basic level: meaning more to every new person you encounter than they could possibly mean to you.

We drive past a billboard advertising Dollywood. I think how exhausting Parton's life would be for a normal person. Parton isn't normal, though. I suspect that after all this time she needs the constant pressure of fame to feel like herself. I say that with no sense of judgment. In fact, I feel only awe in face of Parton's ability to constantly perform under that pressure. She thrives in the spotlight she has built for herself—maybe she feels she couldn't survive without it.

Parton's hotel is called the DreamMore Resort. It is named after the commencement speech that Parton gave at the University of Tennessee in 2009. That speech, where Parton popularized her mantra, "Dream more, learn more, care more, and be more," became a best-selling inspirational book. Remarkably, that book has now become a destination hotel and resort. Dolly moves in remarkable ways.

The resort hotel is the largest part of a $300 million expansion of the Dollywood empire that also gave the theme park a facelift and a couple new roller coasters.[5] The expansion provides, for the first time in Dollywood history, a place for guests to stay. The facility hosts business meetings and weddings and offers full-service dining, as well as a salon and spa. It boasts high-end guest rooms, including Dolly Parton's "Suite Dream," a 2,200-square-foot penthouse complete with décor "inspired by Dolly," according to a 2015 press release. The subtitle of her book *Dream More: Celebrate the Dreamer in You* inspired the early advertising for the resort.

As we go up the lane leading to the parking lot, I'm not thinking about my dreams—I'm still obsessing about how Parton makes it back home. My biggest question is answered almost immediately as we enter the resort grounds and are greeted by Parton's tour bus. The bus is parked in a small enclosure at the edge of the parking lot. Inside the fence is a small tent, set up with a cooler and some modest patio furniture. A golf cart sits nearby, along with a late-model burgundy van emblazoned with Dolly's signature and butterfly logo. There will be a lot of butterflies.

At the front desk my wife asks the clerk if Dolly really stays on her bus while she's here. She nods, adding that Dolly loves the new hotel: "Yesterday she was sitting in that rocker, greeting everyone and singing. It's just so exciting when she's here."

The hotel is tastefully appointed, not over the top, very *Southern Living*. Portraits of Parton are everywhere—like a benevolent Smoky Mountain Mao—as are more butterflies. They cover every available surface. Our room has a large print of a monarch butterfly dancing across a field of flowers. Stitched on an afghan with blue butterflies on it is "'Put wings on your dreams'—Dolly." Even the toilet paper has a little butterfly embossed on it.

Our window has a nice enough view of the Smokies, but it also has a great view of Parton's bus. From our room we can see that the bus is separated from the resort grounds by a large lawn. The lawn is out of the way enough to make it clear when someone is headed to Parton's bus and not just wandering around the grounds. A girl who seems to be about fifteen and her mother are looking at the bus from across the meadow. They have made several false starts at crossing the lawn, so I figure she's nervous. When they finally make it across, they walk around the enclosure several times until a security guard comes out to speak with them. After a short while he disappears into the enclosure and quickly returns to let them in, apparently for an audience with the queen. Later in the afternoon I spot the girl admiring her newly autographed Dolly Parton T-shirt in the lobby.

$\sim$

The first time I went to Dollywood was several years earlier, at the end of the summer of 2011. August in the Smokies can often provide a respite from the rest of the South. Sometimes the temperatures at the higher elevations can be as much as twenty degrees cooler than they are in the muggy piedmont of North Carolina or Tennessee's central basin. But during that particular visit in 2011, there was no respite. The temperatures were well into the 80s. Instead of lowering the temperature, the altitude just made it feel like we were being pressed against the sun. Everyone at Dollywood was sweating, and gasping for air—myself very much included.

Pigeon Forge is often sold as the heart of the mountains, but it's actually comparatively flat. This stretch of land was at one time probably desirable farmland compared with the surrounding hills and hollers—but now that flat ground is used for miniature golf courses, hotels, restaurants, and parking lots. The sun's rays pound directly onto the scalps of those of us waiting our turn for one of the park's rides. Dollywood has plenty of rides—more than forty and adding more every year. They range from roller coasters and water rides to tamer fare like Ferris wheels and a vintage carousel—the kinds of attractions familiar to anybody who has been to a Busch Gardens or a Six Flags or wherever. The rides make it tempting to presume that the park is just another easily digested theme park, one of many rather than a unique place.

On that hot day in August, I made that mistake. Maybe it was the smell of tar from the heat-softened asphalt mingling with the smoke from the barbecue stand and whatever chemical they use to clean the water in the log flume, but I thought I understood Dollywood pretty quickly. See, by my own hazy calculations, I thought that this could be anybody's attraction. Dolly Parton is from Pigeon Forge, so it makes sense that she'd stick her name on a tourist magnet like a theme park. It could be anybody's name on this park, I thought, so the remarkable feature of this place is Parton's fame. That a country singer could be famous enough to support this kind of attraction is a straightforward novelty. After a day at the park I'd concluded that I'd figured the place out: it is a wild and wacky symptom of Dolly Parton's fame.

Rest assured that I was wrong. I hadn't figured anything out at all; in fact, I wasn't even perceptive enough to understand what I didn't know.

If you've ever read something about Dollywood, online or in a travel section of a newspaper, for example, you've probably encountered what I consider one of the great sins of writing about this theme park or anywhere else, for that matter: not meeting the place halfway. Making Dollywood a kitsch joke allows for a couple of punch lines, but it doesn't really get anybody anywhere. Dolly Parton might be funny, but she's no joke.

I stumbled around this trap when I first went to Dollywood and began thinking about the park. Those who dismiss Dollywood as junk will say something like this: "You'll never believe what the mountain folk in East Tennessee have done: they've built a theme park about Dolly Parton! How weird! How kitsch! They've taken a beautiful landscape and dropped a fake thing about a woman who has become a caricature of herself with plastic surgery right in the middle of it." Then maybe the writer, some dope like me, will try to throw in some ironic detachment or perhaps a lame supposition that the joke's really on all these southerners who are basking in Parton's mountain fantasy without realizing how odd the idea of Dollywood sounds.

I'm sorry, but that's all wrong. Dolly Parton says it best herself: "I may look fake, but where it counts I'm real."[6]

The first time I went to Dollywood I was expecting all that. Like many, I had equated Parton's park with the weird surreal world of roadside kitsch. I actually looked forward to chintzy souvenirs. I'm a genuine fan of Parton's career and thought it would be a worthy thing to check off my bucket list in the same way that a stop or two at Graceland during the course of a lifetime seems mandatory to me as a fan of Elvis Presley's.

I had no idea what I was talking about.

Pigeon Forge has plenty of kitsch, camp, and crap. Some of it has to do with Parton, but most of it does not. Don't be fooled into thinking that somehow the locals or the employees or even Dolly Parton herself don't get what's going on in their town. Dollywood is a deliberate place. The choices made there offer a corrective—albeit a gentle one—to both the constant stereotyping of Appalachia and the rampant commercialism of Pigeon Forge and Gatlinburg. To put it another way: Dolly Parton is smarter than I am. She's probably also smarter than you are.

Wherever I looked for irony at Dollywood, I was disappointed. There was no distance, no room for detachment. No hillbillies were winking from behind a moonshine jug or from beneath threadbare straw hats. The souvenirs weren't that crass either. They were just the kind of souvenirs you'd find anywhere. I learned, on that first trip, that it wasn't that nobody here got the joke—it's that there isn't any joke at all. Dollywood isn't a fake place. Obviously, some elements are incredibly artificial. Everything about any theme park is manufactured—it is a created reality after all. But it is very real in its intention to present Dolly Parton's fondness for her home.

There is an expectation that Dollywood's theme is built around Parton's outsized public persona, but this doesn't seem to be the case. I think it would be more accurate to say that the park is built around Parton's imagined idea of the Smoky Mountains.

Clues to this idea appear all over the park. You turn a corner and stumble upon a facade made to look like that of a grocery store. Cas Walker's Super Market is named for the Knoxville television personality who gave a ten-year-old Dolly Parton a spot on his local show. Next door is Red's Diner, named for the Sevierville cafe where a young Parton ate her first hamburger. The diner is just past a restaurant named for Parton's best friend's grandmother—Granny Ogle's Ham 'n' Beans. The crown jewel of this nostalgia is that replica of the Parton family's cabin. A hand-painted sign by the entrance states: "This cabin is a replica of the Parton homeplace where Lee and Avie Lee Parton raised Dolly and her 10 brothers and sisters. The replica cabin was constructed by Dolly's brother Bobby, and the interior was reproduced by her mother Avie Lee. Most of the items on display are original family treasures. The original cabin still stands at its location in Locust Ridge."

Imagine all those children crowding those rooms and bursting onto the porch. Imagine Avie Lee. What can it possibly have been like to decorate that house? Remember, two rooms and *eleven* children. She was showing the world how relatively few possessions she had—this is a poor family. Avie Lee wasn't just performing poverty for Dollywood's audience though. She was also showing how far she'd come—in the center of her daughter's multimillion-dollar dreamland. Avie Lee is gone now. Her husband is too. But members of the Parton family still perform at Dollywood. Parton relatives have been featured at Dollywood as long as Dolly has been associated with it (she became a partner in the park in 1986, twenty-five years after its first incarnation as a tourist attraction, Rebel Railroad). Lately you can see her younger siblings Cassie and Randy Parton lead a troupe of nieces and cousins through Dolly's songbook. Dolly is ever present, projected on a movie theater–sized screen. During the performance the Parton relatives interact with the twenty-foot virtual Dolly as though she were on stage with them: they laugh together, banter, she sings along, and even laughs at, the performers' carefully scripted jokes.

That show is called *My People*, and it is one of the dozens of shows performed at Dollywood each day. In fact, Dollywood has more performances than any theme park in America—specifically, more than Disneyland.[7]

Music is everywhere. Dollywood employs entertainers to staff all those shows—at least a dozen depending on the seasonal lineup. Most are hired locally, meaning from Knoxville, Asheville, and Chattanooga, so there are lots of aspiring country singers. They sing and dance their way through pleasantly competent medleys of country classics and gospel numbers. Dollywood's street performers barely try to convince the crowds that their studied banter and dances with remarkably complex choreography are somehow spontaneous explosions of nostalgia. The biggest act, maybe even including that of Parton's siblings, is the Kingdom Heirs, a gospel quartet that has been performing at the park in some form since before it was known as Dollywood. Unlike the other performers, the Kingdom Heirs maintain something of an identity outside the park. They release albums, which often make the Christian music charts, and when the park is closed for the season they maintain a touring schedule.

The performers who aren't part of a touring band are left to their own devices in the off-season; they find work in dinner theaters, on cruise ships, and with repertory companies. Others leave for good to try moving up the ladder in Nashville or maybe even on Broadway.

Like the Disney parks or any number of imitators, Dollywood is divided into subregions. These thematic areas represent the different aspects of Appalachian identity and nostalgia that the park traffics in. At Thunderhead Gap, for instance, you can find nods to Appalachian industry: the Thunderhead, a wooden coaster, whips through the area between two mountains where an old sawmill turned logs into lumber. Another roller coaster, the Tennessee Tornado, runs through an area evocative of mining. Jukebox Junction, on the other hand, is where you'll find 1950s nostalgia. This section has the burger place and the Lightning Rod, the fastest wooden roller coaster in the world, with cars that look like hot rods. The country fair has a permanent midway with ring toss, darts, and a Ferris wheel. Craftsman's Valley has no rides; its attractions are—as the name indicates—the blacksmiths, leather workers, carvers, potters, glassblowers, and various other artisans who demonstrate their crafts and interact with park patrons. Unlike, say, Colonial Williamsburg, the artisans at Dollywood aren't playing characters, despite their old-fashioned dress. I once asked a glassblower how he liked life at the park. His answer was candid, current, and concise: "This is one of the only places I know of where I can make a good salary blowing glass."

Craftsman's Valley is also home to the park's chapel. The white chapel is modeled loosely after the Primitive Baptist churches found in the mountains. Probably not by accident, it is similar to the country church in Cades Cove, a popular lush green valley located about ninety minutes away in the Great Smoky Mountains National Park. Dollywood's chapel is a functioning church with Sunday services offered by an evangelical minister. Like other sights at the park, the chapel recalls a piece of Parton's biography. It's named after Robert F. Thomas, the doctor who delivered her and for whom she named her medical foundation.

The Owens Farm section of the park has a lot of rides, including a giant swinging arm called the Barnstormer, sponsored by the Tennessee Farmers Cooperative, that swings riders nearly vertical in an effort to mimic the sensations felt by the stunt pilots of the 1920s.

Dollywood offers lots of things to buy, plenty of restaurants, and the previously mentioned shows and rides. But these can be found in any number of tourist destinations all over the country. What stick out here are the personal touches: the chapel and the cabin, as well as notes and slogans from Parton that hang all over the park. It also has lots of trees. Unlike, say, Disney World, where every hill was carefully planned and every tree selectively forced onto the flatlands of central Florida, the rolling hills and tall old-growth trees at Dollywood feel almost—dare I say?—authentic.

The oldest section of Dollywood, like much of Craftsman's Valley, actually predates Parton's involvement with the park. It is called the Village and throughout its life has represented a Civil War–era town and a Wild West encampment. Now it has kind of a Victorian feel. I have a hard time putting my finger on exactly what the aesthetic is here, as I do for many areas of Dollywood. The Village is sort of like an 1890s ice cream parlor or maybe a riverboat casino or a Victorian bordello—at any rate it looks like the kind of place where sleeve garters and gaslights might fit in. Most important, the Village is home to Dollywood's most famous ride: the train.

The Dollywood Express, cars pulled by one of several steam locomotives, was originally built for the US Army in 1943. Called Klondike Katie in those days, its engines carried troops and supplies from Whitehorse, the capital of Canada's Yukon Territory, to Skagway, Alaska, during World War II. The coal-burning engines have been used in Pigeon Forge since 1961. The locomotive winds through most of Dollywood's neighborhoods. From it you can see the gristmill, which sits at the edge of Craftsman's Valley and sells cornmeal ground on site (as well as popular sweets), and the Wild Eagle, a roller coaster that towers over the park.

If butterflies represent Parton's ideal of natural beauty (serene, colorful, delicate, "rare and gentle things"), her passion for eagles represents the beauty of the wild. Opened in 2012, the Wild Eagle was marketed as America's first winged roller coaster, a ride created by a Swiss company that puts the rider, sitting on a giant sculpted eagle's wing, alongside the track with nothing above or below. The ride also takes full advantage of the park's topography: it sits at one of Dollywood's highest points, providing the rider with a spectacular view—which turns into a blur when your eagle goes into a two-hundred-foot dive at sixty miles an hour.

Parton's fondness for raptors is evident in one of the park's long-running shows, "The Wings of America" bird show, a celebration of birds of prey presented by a not-for-profit organization called the American Eagle Foundation. The foundation has performance space at the park, where it houses several rehabilitated bald eagles that, for various reasons, cannot be returned to the wild. A parade of hawks, owls, vultures, and assorted other birds perform tricks while the audience learns about raptors. The star of the show, the bald eagle, appears for the grand finale while a patriotic montage is projected on a screen on stage. The host, a friendly-faced fellow named Mike Acuff, who is dressed in a Jack Hanna–style outfit, wears a stiff leather glove used by bird handlers and holds the eagle up for the audience, which applauds. Then, improbably, Acuff begins to sing. "Fly eagle fly," he sings to the bird while propping one leg on a tree stump, "go spread your freedom wings across our sky."[8]

$\sim$

I'm at Dollywood again. A different time—different visit. This is a particularly important trip for me (but not for anybody else). It's the first time I'm here specifically to do research for a series of projects on Dollywood that will eventually become this book. It's not as hot, so I'm comfortable wearing long pants and dress shoes—which I bought the day before at the Sevierville outlet mall. I'm trying to take myself seriously in the hope that the people I'm interviewing will do the same.

The day before I do my interviews I decide to walk around Dollywood for several hours to take notes and gather my thoughts. I do a couple of laps of the park. The gospel museum is empty. It's been quiet most times I've been in there, but today I have it all to myself. When you enter the museum, you walk into a room built to look like a chapel. A slightly terrifying animatronic quartet sings hymns. Everything smells a little like wax. The gift shop, operated by the Southern Gospel Music Association, is having a sale of vinyl records. The only artist I recognize is Bill Gaither, an Indiana gospel magnate who still draws huge crowds for his homecomings. The gift shop also sells those shirts that take familiar brand logos and make them about Jesus, for example, in the style of Reese's Peanut Butter Cups: "Jesus: Sweet Savior." They have dozens.

I step out of the gospel museum and back into sunlight. I walk up the hill toward the roller coasters. The park's sound system is playing Parton's cover of "Shine." I say with no sense of irony, distance, or provocation that it is a brilliant, beautiful, and true recording. Originally the song was a staple of mid-1990s college rock radio, written and performed by a Georgia alternative rock band, Collective Soul. Parton sings on a more human scale than the original, more restrained. She makes it sound almost like a church song. If you haven't heard it, listen to it now—I'll be here when you get back.

~

After I make my way around the roller coasters, I find myself walking down the other side of the hill toward Craftsman's Valley. I've often lingered in this part of the park, but this time I notice something I never noticed before. The leather worker's store has a small display window, and there with the belts, wallets, and bags are a couple of National Rifle Association shirts. This poses problems for me in a couple of ways. Although this was the first time I'd noticed the shirts, I had a feeling (later confirmed) that these shirts had been for sale there for quite some time. This meant I probably hadn't been paying close enough attention on previous visits. It also forced me to entertain an idea that quite honestly I didn't want to ponder: that Dolly Parton has built a red-state Disneyland.

I live in the South, in North Carolina, and have for some time. But I didn't grow up there—I was born and raised in Indiana. It's probably fair to say that people in both states are generally comfortable with the idea of gun ownership. Many in these states—and much of the South and the Midwest—own guns, often zealously. And while I don't want to explore the gun rights debate here, I would argue that gun culture, hunting culture, or whatever you want to call it isn't quite the same thing as the NRA. The NRA is, in point of fact, a political organization. It lobbies, campaigns, and endorses an agenda designed to forward the interests of gun makers. The NRA, in other words, is politics. I know: everything is politics, but the NRA is *really* politics. It's politics on steroids.

So why does this bother me? It's not that it bothers my Chapel Hill sensibility or that counternarratives disturb my own political views, though both are probably true. What really bothers me about the NRA shirts above all else is that they complicate my idea of Dollywood.

In truth, my worries about Dollywood's being a red-state Disney—it isn't—last only a split second. I guess, if anything, red-state Disney is just one of many roles the park plays. Donald Trump won Sevier County handily, and the bumper stickers and T-shirts you see around here tell you that wasn't a surprise. But I don't think that's the whole story.

Dollywood isn't just a safe place for the Right. Among its other roles are gay vacation destination, family-friendly retreat, home base for Dolly Parton fanatics, place for church camp kids to ride roller coasters, home for artisans, and place for working musicians to get a toehold on a career. Giving any of those facets priority over any other would be a mistake. It is a complex place, a living place.

$\sim$

One of my favorite things at Dollywood is not a ride or an activity or a show. It is Dolly Parton's personal museum, Chasing Rainbows. It houses all manner of Parton ephemera. Most affecting to me are the photographs from very, very early in her career. Right around when she made that move to Nashville and just before it. One photo is from her senior class trip to the 1964 New York World's Fair. On the way back to Tennessee she and her classmates stopped in Washington and took a photo of all the seniors on the National Mall. There she is in the center of the group but somehow apart. Her hair, or maybe her wig, has already found its shade of blonde, and she's almost got the Dolly Parton makeup down. She's creating herself, as all high school seniors do. But even early in what would be a very public life, there's something special there. I guess it's what people mean when they refer to star power.

If you take a walk through the towns of Sevier County, it is fun to imagine a teenage Dolly Parton soldiering through, knowing she was meant for greatness, and maybe distracting herself from that inexorable pull of stardom by being just a teenager driving around with her cousin: "We used to cruise Gatlinburg or Sevierville, circling the Tastee-Freez, flirting with the boys, and singing. I'd always carry my guitar. Most of the girls around there were kind of shy, and I would always manage to attract the boys with my singing and joking."[9]

What is it like to grow up to be famous or important? What is it like to go from so poor to so rich? What is it like to live in the public eye as a kind of exaggerated impersonation of yourself? What is it like to not just leave a mark on the place you're from but to change it forever?

For me these questions hold a lesson, a message we can learn from Dolly Parton and her homeland. I think that for all its plastic detritus, Dollywood actually shows a profound connection to its place. From that we can learn a willingness not to let our homes and our backgrounds define us but to also accept the challenge to define where we come from. Dolly Parton's success also tells us to embrace life, to say yes. Nothing about Pigeon Forge can be seen as pessimistic, and this may not always work to its advantage. But disregarding pessimism and allowing good things to happen to you has value, even if those good things sometimes also bring tacky wax museums and taffy stores.

So how did all this get here? Did Parton really rebuild her hometown? To answer these questions I think it's helpful to look at the history of this place. It's hard to believe now, but people didn't start coming to Sevier County because Dolly Parton was born there. In fact, people have been vacationing there for generations. And the closer I look, the more I begin to wonder how the place and the persona have influenced each other. I begin to wonder how this place became the destination it is today and what role Dolly Parton played in that transformation. Her influence over the town is easy to see today, but how did growing up here influence her? If people were coming here before Parton, how did that affect her? Has Pigeon Forge been shaped by Dolly or has Pigeon Forge shaped Dolly?

Rebels, Tourists, and a
Tennessee Mountain Home

I want to come back here and build something special to honor my people.

—Dolly Parton[1]

WHILE I'M visiting Pigeon Forge, it strikes me as a place that doesn't seem to revere its history. This is not particularly remarkable. Americans tend to be fascinated largely with our newness. In most American places the next thing takes priority over whatever came before. Maybe this is different in Europe or Asia, where there seems to be a perception of long, uninterrupted narratives. I suspect that those narratives have more to do with self-mythologizing than with history, but perception matters.

History is an attempt to find truth in memory, and memory is an attempt to find narrative in time. Moments slip past us and we try to figure out what they meant and where we've been. Historians see the narratives we make—our memories—as too tied to our emotions and sense of self to be reliable.

The factual aspects of history are important—and they are provable. Someone was born on this date, and at this time a bomb was dropped or a love letter was sent. These are the almost mathematical truths that historians build their work on. These are also the most boring parts of history. Motivations, memories, perceptions—the narratives are the interesting parts. Whether a narrative is true is impossible to know, because we all perceive reality in our own way. Perception is as factual—and as unreliable—as taste.

Akira Kurosawa's film *Rashomon* (1950) provides the most famous example of the subjectivity of truth. The movie shows four different version of a crime as told by four different witnesses and participants. The multiple realities are never resolved, and what the truth is is never made explicit. This storytelling device has become associated with the film to the point of cliché. "The *Rashomon* effect" shows up in other films, sitcoms, serials, cartoons, and anywhere else that a storyteller wants to imbue a sense of ambiguity.[2]

Here's the thing—the multifaceted ambiguity of *Rashomon* isn't just a storytelling device for fiction—it is suitable for any narrative. Even history. Even books about Dollywood.

If it sounds as if I'm making some kind of posttruth, artifact argument here, I'm not. At the risk of oversimplification, all I'm really saying is that the truth is complicated. I should confess that I take no comfort in this. Accepting other narratives can be discomfiting, especially when they're waving Confederate flags, but I'll get to that later. (I want to make it especially clear that, as far as I know, Dolly Parton doesn't wave Confederate flags, and if she ever has, I would be surprised—she doesn't seem like the type.)

I think that thinking about narrative is helpful when you look at the way Pigeon Forge presents history (and when it doesn't).[3] It is easy to imagine that Dolly Parton is the starting point for the history of Pigeon Forge—that she created the place with the sheer force of her celebrity—but she didn't. She is actually part of a long trajectory of mountain tourism that stretches back decades, even centuries. I'll look at some startling places that use pre-Dolly history—and the questions I have about what that version of history is trying to tell us. Also, every book about the South seems to have a chapter that talks about the Confederate flag—this is that chapter.

~

Parton, her park, and her persona cast an awfully long shadow over the mountains. Her universal acclaim and status as beloved favorite daughter also help weave her inextricably into the cultural fabric of East Tennessee. She has become so inextricably linked to the region that some of Parton's fans may find it easy to believe that mountain tourism originates with her. I understand the feeling. In Pigeon Forge and Gatlinburg Dolly is so omnipresent that it's hard to imagine a tourist industry without her.

In fact, the roots of tourism in the Appalachian Mountains don't originate with Parton. Instead, they date closer to the turn of the nineteenth century. With independence firmly established, the new American government turned its attention to the West. In southern Appalachia both the terrain and the relatively large indigenous population served as initial deterrents for white expansion west. While the terrain was seen as a permanent obstacle, the federal government felt that the existing Native American population was movable. The first three decades of the 1800s saw a forced expulsion of the original Appalachian population. The vast empty wilderness of nineteenth-century North Carolina and Tennessee was not a natural creation; in fact it was the result of a systematic federal depopulation program.

Cherokee Chief John Ross, the son of a Scots-Cherokee mother and a Scottish father, fought the removal at the Supreme Court and before Congress. Ross was able to move through white society with relative ease. He had traveled extensively, traded throughout the south, and served in the military. He also owned slaves, an important signifier of elite status in Andrew Jackson's America. He wore European clothes—not surprising since he was seven-eighths European.

Ross put an acute focus on the Cherokee removal. He made it a legal struggle rather than an issue of westernization or the taming of wilderness. His ability to meet white politicians on their terms showed the practice for what is was—a racially motivated land grab. His argument worked, on some. Davy Crockett, then congressman from Tennessee (who now has a distillery named in his honor in Gatlinburg), called Indian removal a "wicked, unjust measure."[4]

Despite Ross's prolonged legal protestations, soldiers hunted native families and marched them on a prolonged journey that would eventually land them in Oklahoma.[5] Some families were split up and many native people died. The route would eventually become commonly known as the Trail of Tears.[6] It was one of the most staggering acts of ethnic cleansing committed by the US government. This deliberate act of erasure—the violent creation of wilderness—would be the first of many impositions on these mountains of an imagined narrative.

It is important to remember these removals as a kind of base for our cultural conception of Appalachia today. In Pigeon Forge and Gatlinburg, which have no greater business than selling an idea of the mountains, you find little mention of the natives who were forced west. At her attractions Dolly Parton has tried to do a little better. She has paid tribute to the Cherokee in a show at Dollywood, "Sha-Kon-O-Hey! Land of Blue Smoke," and the Indians get a passing mention in her dinner theater production, *The Dixie Stampede*. These gestures serve only as reminders of how little of the story is actually getting told. In Sevier County the erasure has been largely successful—and startlingly permanent.

Across the mountains in Cherokee, North Carolina, is an interesting exception to this narrative. The Eastern Band of the Cherokee Indians has maintained a strong cultural presence there, including ownership of tribal land. Like Pigeon Forge and Gatlinburg, the reservation has been a magnet for tourists; they come for Native American arts and crafts and, more recently, for the Harrah's Casino, which hosts the largest hotel in North Carolina.[7]

After the natives had been removed from the rest of the mountains, white settlers quickly moved to fill the empty wilderness. Following on the heels of the first waves of permanent settlement were proto-tourists, members of the elite planter class, who sought refuge in the cooler mountain air from the heat and humidity of the Carolina piedmont and Low Country. Accommodating the tourists were the progenitors of mountain resorts: inns and lodges, often built around the natural sulfur springs that were said to have curative powers.

On the Tennessee side of the Appalachian Mountains, these springs tended to attract planters from the Deep South. By the 1850s the aristocratic classes from Tennessee's own central basin, as well as from states like Louisiana and Mississippi, were soon luxuriating in hotels and lodges like Beersheba Springs in Blount County and Montvale Spring in Grundy County.[8] Similar resorts that popped up on the North Carolina side of the mountains drew from the large planter class of Virginia, South Carolina, and Georgia. They had prospered by managing plantations of cotton, tobacco, and indigo and ranked as some of the wealthiest citizens in the relatively new republic. As development spread, the wealthy planters who visited East Tennessee became more geographically diverse.

All this seems light years away from present-day Pigeon Forge. A few minutes on the Pigeon Forge Parkway tells any observer that this destination no longer is intended for the elite, although some locales in the mountains still cater to the one percent. At Blackberry Farm, a resort just twenty-five miles southwest of Pigeon Forge, the emphasis is on luxurious farm-to-table ingredients and the ability to offer discreet comfort to celebrity guests. An average room there will run you about $900 a night—assuming you can get a reservation.[9] While the farm-fresh meals have made it a destination for well-heeled foodies, its air of mountain authenticity and exclusive price point have made it Tennessee's go-to spot for celebrity weddings; country music brides like Kelly Clarkson and Ashley Monroe have tied the knot there. Blackberry Farm and its antecedents counter the notion that Appalachian culture has been tied to—and tied up by—isolation. After all, how isolated could this place really be when the wealthiest vacationers in the United States have been tramping over these mountains for the past 150 years? If anything, any cultural separation that may have occurred in the Smoky Mountains resulted from class stratification, not hillbillies hiding from progress in the woods.

The wealthy and influential vacationers from Virginia, the Carolinas, and the Mississippi delta brought with them the fraught race and class consciousness of the antebellum period. They also brought their slaves. Wealthy visitors to the mountains found local levels of poverty distasteful and were largely uninterested in the mountain communities around their holiday havens.

By the eve of the Civil War most of the fancy facilities excluded local residents both as guests and employees. They dismissed local cooks and staff in favor of the enslaved workforce brought by the vacationers.[10] This laid the foundation for locals' profound ambivalence, and on occasion outright hostility, toward the institutions of the Old South, especially slavery.

This stratification caused a rift between the mountain people and the Southern gentry that became increasingly acute as the Civil War became inevitable. To put it bluntly, the mountain folk felt no particular inclination to fight—and to die—to preserve the Southern way of life. "I'm not from the South," a friend from western North Carolina once told me. "I'm from the mountains first, then maybe I'm a southerner, then an American, and so on, but the mountains and the South—those can be different places." I don't know if this is true for everybody in the mountains, but it makes sense to me.

In 1863 Lucy French, a visitor to Beersheba Springs, near what is today the South Cumberland State Park, wrote of the locals living near her vacation destination: "Yesterday we rode out to see some of the mountain people. I do say I could have never imagined that people could live so." French is not as galled by the mountaineers' apparent poverty as by their apparent lack of an inferiority complex: "The strangest thing to me was that they showed no embarrassment, but appeared to think themselves all right and just as good as anybody living."[11] These lines sound as if they could have been written by someone covering Bobby Kennedy's trip to Appalachia in the 1960s or, more recently, by a journalist writing an exposé of poverty in coal country. Some things seem to stay the same.

Today it's easy to imagine Appalachian opposition to secession as progressivism. Just as we like to imagine that Dolly Parton's strategic political silences mean she aligns with our positions, we imagine that the anti-Confederate sentiment of Parton's home county came from an overriding sense of mountain decency. This plays out in some of the explanations for Appalachian Republicanism. Was it that they were too poor to own slaves? Or maybe it was the strong sense of Christian justice that still courses through the region. Or perhaps the poor highlanders understood what it meant to be a member of the antebellum underclass. Parts of any of these ideas might be a little true, but the record shows that the residents of East Tennessee probably didn't care much about slavery, and when they did take a stance, it was usually a supportive one.[12]

In other words, it probably wasn't that the mountaineers sided with the enslaved people; it was that they didn't particularly like the enslavers.

When war did break out, many of the men of fighting age in Sevier County chose to fight *against* their home state. They would travel up the mountains to Kentucky and enlist in the Union Army there.[13] This bit of history feels particularly disjointed today, when the rebel flag waves in the yards of area homes and flies from the beds of pickups cruising the Pigeon Forge Parkway. The people who voted against and fought against what that flag stood for now seem totally lost.

With the defeat of the Confederacy, the leisured lifestyle cultivated by the Southern planters largely crumbled. Much of the wealth had dried up in the war effort, a generation of young men was decimated, and slavery—the mechanism by which the planters had exerted their power—was now illegal. The conflict had left many patrons of East Tennessee's antebellum resorts destitute or dead. It also seems likely that planters would have been disinclined to return to a region that had frequently been hostile to their cause.

The evaporation of the antebellum tourism industry in the mountains primed Appalachia for its mythic status as a lost place. The white supremacist class system of chattel slavery was economically exploitative and shaped mountain resorts, but they created a dialog, however unequal, between Appalachia and the rest of the South. In the postbellum period that discussion ended, which caused people to begin to imagine Appalachia as a region apart.

After the Civil War and the drop in mountain tourism, Sevier County's economy relied heavily on agriculture well into the twentieth century. Industry made sporadic appearances, but few such concerns lived long. Railroad service came to the county in 1905, and it, along with steamship service on the Little Pigeon River, provided shipping for the timber industry.[14] Several other small factories opened around Sevierville in the first decades of the twentieth century, including a cheese factory cooperative owned by a group of local farmers, but none had a lasting economic impact. Sevier County's most significant early factory, the Stokely Canning Factory, was built in 1926. By the thirties timber was dwindling as a result of deforestation and in some part because of pressure from conservationists.[15]

A desire to preserve the natural landscape of the mountains came about, somewhat perversely, because of the introduction of the automobile. Cars brought people into the mountains on short excursions. These early motoring tourists had a desire to maintain the scenic land that they enjoyed. The historian Anne Whisnant tells us that the growth of the national park system "was inextricably tied to the spread of cars and the growth of tourism."[16] Although the parks were created to preserve natural landscapes, behind this agenda was an unmistakable desire to create attractions. Stephen Mather, the first director of the National Park Service, believed it was essential that a park be "accessible and popular."[17]

Like Dolly Parton, who wanted to create a version of the Smoky Mountains that tourists could immerse themselves in, National Park Service administrators wanted to create a real space out of an imaginary. The historian Richard D. Starnes writes that the National Park Service created its own Smoky Mountain fantasy by privileging landscape over history, "In creating an idealized landscape that minimized the historical realities of settlement, logging, mining, and other activities, park leaders created a visitor experience in which the park became a place where land could be viewed and enjoyed without the complications of human experience."[18]

The Great Smoky Mountains National Park, like Dollywood, is a created landscape. The park is typically seen as a pristine wilderness, when, in fact, it is a wilderness curated with an eye for authenticity. The creation—not one without controversy—is a piece of the park that is allowed to remain wild while surrounded by developed land.

In *Super-Scenic Motorway,* a history of the Blue Ridge Parkway, Whisnant describes the often-contentious creation of the public preserves:
"Severe controversy arose . . . over the Park Service's policy of removing all residents from parklands to re-create the image of pristine wilderness."[19] The politics of removal became acts of creation. The park
service removes species that are not native species and restricts the behavior of visitors and businesses in the park. As the federal government
forced out original residents of the parkland, it made careful decisions
about which structures, signs of human life, would remain.[20] Similarly,
Starnes argues that this national park "is an artificial creation of space,
landscape, and history defined by those charged with its care and those
who visit."[21]

By the early sixties Interstate 40 and US 441 connected in Knoxville,
a pivotal crossroads. The interstate brought people from the East and
West, and US 441 connected those travelers with Florida, but first they
had to pass through Sevier County. The increase in automobile traffic
led to interest in developing the tourist trade. Gatlinburg, the community that directly borders the national park, was a natural choice. Sight-
seers had stayed there since the founding of the park in the 1930s, and
Gatlinburg had maintained a high degree of local ownership until the
eighties.[22] Seeking an area in which to gain a foothold during the postwar tourism boom, outside investors turned to Pigeon Forge, an un-
incorporated community between Gatlinburg and the county seat of
Sevierville. The rush of tourist development led to the incorporation
of the town in 1961.[23] Within a few years property values inflated by
the development of tourist attractions had pushed multigenerational
farming families out of Pigeon Forge.[24]

The Robbins brothers built Rebel Railroad, the first theme park
to occupy the land that is now Dollywood, in 1961. The brothers also
founded the Tweetsie Railroad, western North Carolina's longest-lived
theme park (it opened in 1957 and still welcomes visitors today). Rebel
Railroad featured a ride through the mountains that included a staged
assault on a train by "Yankee raiders." After the faux Confederate
troops repelled the faux Union troops, the ride ended at a Confederate village that featured a blacksmith, a restaurant, and a handful of
other attractions. According to the historian C. Brenden Martin, "Rebel

Railroad was ahistorical, contradicting the area's strong Union sentiment during the Civil War."[25] The contradiction became more extreme when Art Modell, the then-owner of the Cleveland Browns, purchased Rebel Railroad and morphed the park into a Wild West village. The Yankees became Indians and the Confederate village was reimagined a thousand miles west. Its name was changed from Rebeltown to Goldrush Junction.[26]

~

The popular imagination of the eighteenth through twentieth centuries, and, it appears, the twenty-first century, has liked to think of the Appalachian mountains as a region of almost desperate isolation. For most of the twentieth century that isolation was more fiction than reality. Timber and coal, as well as tourism, attracted to the region not only railroads that connected it to the wider regional and global networks but also many inhabitants, who came to cut wood, dig coal, and work a variety of other jobs available in industrial Appalachia. Additionally, the railroads—among other modes of transportation—made it easier for mountain residents to move out. As the folklorist D. K. Wilgus pointed out, in 1970 the white and black settlers who made the mountains their home didn't get stuck there like mosquitoes in amber. "It would be more accurate to note," Wilgus writes, "that the settlers not only went where they did because they wanted to go, but stayed there because they wanted to stay. They could have left. Many of them did, and many of them returned."[27] Those who returned from places like Pittsburgh, Detroit, and Gary, Indiana, brought back an awareness of how the rest of the country viewed the mountains.

The absorption of a popular Appalachian identity through migrations shaped the way residents of East Tennessee presented themselves to outsiders and to each other. The former southerners maintained mountain culture in absentia, particularly through music. Whether they were Kentuckians who listened to familiar old-time music on the Chicago-based *National Barn Dance* (WLS radio, 1924–60; WGN radio, 1960–68) or supported Bill Monroe, the founder of bluegrass music, whose early performances were in Hammond, Indiana. Monroe himself wasn't from the mountains; he was from Rosine, in western Kentucky. Monroe understood the appeal of mountain music, though, and borrowed liberally from Appalachian sources like the Carter Family to create his style.[28]

Transplanted Appalachians might have heard Monroe and his evocations of their home or they may have watched the *Beverly Hillbillies* (1962–71) or read *Li'l Abner* (1934–77) or seen *Deliverance* (1972), all of which colored their perception of what home meant to the world at large. This feedback loop gave outside creators a surprising opportunity to define what mountain culture meant, even among people who lived, or had lived, in the region. In some cases the depictions were reverential and likely a source of esteem (Monroe). In others the depictions were less helpful (*Deliverance*).

The business of tourism, as a form of capital and cultural expression, permeates every aspect of the cultural identity of the mountain South, particularly in East Tennessee and western North Carolina. "Tourist operators recognized the appeal of mountain culture to tourists and developed diverse methods to profit from it," writes Starnes in *Creating the Land of the Sky*.[29] Tourism has existed in the Smokies for more than two hundred years and has surpassed logging, agriculture, and manufacturing to become a primary industry in the mountains.[30] Despite its ties to fun, pleasure, and leisure, tourism is a deeply expressive realm of American life. What we do for fun is a window into who we are.

Ironically, the expansion of tourism led to worries that a Yogi Berra–style problem was developing: so many people were coming to the mountains that no one would want to come anymore. Of chief concern was that tourists would wipe out the region's prime asset: its unique natural and cultural landscape. According to the historian Jane Becker, this led to an interesting tension, one of simultaneous development and preservation.[31]

C. Brenden Martin argues that the first attraction that brought visitors to East Tennessee by car was the Pi Beta Phi sorority's Arrowmont School for Arts and Crafts, founded in 1912, which quickly became a magnet for middle-class tourists looking for souvenirs of supposedly authentic mountain culture.[32] Becker notes that the Pi Beta

Phi settlement school, and the others that quickly followed, asserted themselves as arbiters between people who lived in the mountains and their middle-class, white American audience: the schools "called on Appalachian craftspeople to use their skills to interpret not their own values and customs, but the culture of others."[33] Women led most of these tourism efforts. In *Beyond Hill and Hollow,* Elizabeth Engelhardt demonstrates that women were the central figures in creating these schools, such as Hindman in Kentucky, as well as the field of Appalachian studies. These early scholars studied what was often considered women's work, such as textiles, crafts, and foodways, in an effort to create a narrative about the "local color" of the Appalachian Mountains.[34]

"Local color" refers to writing that highlights the customs, accents, and culture of a place. At the dawn of the twentieth century, with a new modern world on the horizon, some literary giants looked to preserve regionalisms that they feared would be lost to modernism. Today what they were seeking might be called the "real America." Joel Chandler Harris, Kate Chopin, and even Mark Twain all looked to record life in the South in their day. According to Becker, "Local color fiction writers convinced urban Americans that the mountaineers were sturdy Anglo-Saxon peoples maintaining noble values and traditions—in music, language, dance, and domestic arts—that had disappeared with the onslaught of industry elsewhere in the country."[35]

At their best these texts, despite their warts, can be an invaluable source for anthropologists and folklorists. The writers often favored difference over commonalities and were prone to caricature and stereotype. The notion of purity celebrated by the local colorists—as well as early folklorists like Horace Kephart—was a fantasy. Of course, the white mountaineers were not native to the mountains, a distinction that belonged to the Creek and the Yuchi—and later the Cherokee.[36] Nor were Anglo-Saxons alone in finding a home in the mountains. They shared mountain life with a few African Americans, eastern and southern European immigrants, and the triracial Melungeons—among others. The often-overlooked diversity of southern Appalachia continues today with more recent influxes of immigrants from India, Southeast Asia, and Latin America—not to mention the hippies, communalists,

and folklorists who have found mountain homes since the countercultural revolutions of the 1960s.[37]

~

History is complicated. It is thorny and often uncomfortable. Fantasy,
by design, is easier. Dolly Parton is really good at fantasy. Nowhere
is this more evident than at her humongous, ridiculous, and almost
hilarious and inadvertently complicated venue, the Dixie Stampede
Dinner Attraction. Opened in 1988, the venue was built to capitalize
on Dollywood's then-recent but widespread success. The Stampede,
which is not part of Dollywood, was also an attempt by Parton and her
business partners, Herschend Family Entertainment, to build on the
growth of a variety of entertainment businesses on the Pigeon Forge
Parkway. Comedy theaters, biblical extravaganzas, wax museums, and
miniature golf courses were multiplying just outside Dollywood's
door. So, Parton and her team decided to join the fray.

The Stampede is a modern Wild West show with buffalo, horses, riding tricks, and stunts set to a vaguely Civil War–themed extravaganza—
the North versus the South.

The show begins in a saloon with a three-piece bluegrass band and
comedy act called Mountain Ruckus. Servers, called "Dixie Belles" in
the promotional materials, bring guests popcorn and soft drinks. Like
Dollywood and most of Pigeon Forge, the Dixie Stampede is completely dry. When Mountain Ruckus finishes warming up the crowd,
the audience is escorted into the main arena. The audience is divided
in two, one side representing the North and the other side the South.
The (enormous) dining room/theater space is lit to look like twilight,
and the sound system pipes in the calls of crickets and frogs. The vast,
two-thousand seat venue surrounds a dirt performance area.[38] Surrounding it are benches behind long communal tables. At the head of
the room is a two-story facade of the manor house of a white Georgian
plantation. The décor is literally moonlight and magnolias.

At one point in the show an aerial acrobat dressed as a thunderbird-
like creature performs a routine that purports to honor the Cherokee, "who first inhabited these mountains." Later, after the Native

Americans vanish in favor of pioneers and covered wagons, we're told about the differences between North and South. The North, we are told, is a land of industry, big cities, and the Statue of Liberty. The South, on the other hand, is a place of dreams.

Joan Stack, curator of art collections at the State Historical Society of Missouri, describes the difference in a review of the show. While the traditions of the North are described in a few sentences, the troupe performs Southern traditions for the audience: "Southern belles in hooped skirts twirl on a floating gazebo, their dresses lighting up as they spin. Beneath them, a Southern 'gentleman' rides in, wearing a white suit illuminated with fairy lights. His horse begins walking sideways in an elegant 'dressage' performance that ends with the animal 'bowing' to the audience. Slaves are excluded from this idealized vision of southern bliss."[39] Southern gents and belles aren't re-creations of anything anymore. Instead they're a collection of fantasies from various generations. Like an urban legend, our collective idea of Southern belles is so powerful that it doesn't need history or reality to exist.

Like the Rebel Railroad, this performance of history contradicts the actual history of the county. If you are sitting in that stadium-cum-dining room, it's a little too easy to ignore that most of East Tennessee was staunchly pro-Union and Sevier County was no exception. Fewer than 4 percent of the county's residents voted in favor of secession, and the longtime abolitionist sentiments of the population led to a free black population of significant size.[40] The continued erasure of this history is reminiscent of what the historian and author Timothy Tyson describes in North Carolina: "There's no memory that white people opposed the Civil War." He also notes, "[We] reinvent a fake history for ourselves that doesn't deal with the complexities. . . . So that the kind of self-congratulatory history that passes for heritage keeps us from seeing ourselves and doing better."[41] For some of Parton's fans this kind of historicism is troubling. Bothered by the show's "dishonest history," Helen Morales, a British writer and historian, writes of her trip to Dixie Stampede, "I had not reckoned on being confronted so directly with America, American history, American values . . . nor had I anticipated feeling less close, an aversion even to Dolly Parton as a result."[42]

In recent years some Civil War aspects of the Dixie Stampede have been toned down slightly. The first flag of the Confederacy was removed from the signage and the servers' uniforms have shifted from the stylized Union and Confederate costumes they once wore to more generic blue-and-gray Old West ensembles. In many ways these changes fail to eliminate controversy. The hard reality of a show like Dixie Stampede is that the obfuscation of the history is the problem, and further measures to try to minimize the impact of that history serve only to highlight the question: Why choose this for the subject of a dinner show at all? In January 2015 Parton and her partners announced that the Dixie Stampede would undergo an overhaul. Parton said, "My team is hard at work creating a new set, powerful new music, lots of amazing special effects and a few other surprises."[43] It is hard to imagine that this spectacle will continue to be weighed down by a Confederate fantasy. It seems inevitable that Parton and her team will continue to move in a less contentious direction.

∽

In 1860 the census showed that 538 slaves—about 6 percent of the total population—were living in Sevier County. This number is far lower than for the state of Tennessee as a whole, where 26 percent of the population was enslaved.[44]

Although enslaved people represented a much smaller percentage of the Sevier County population than they did elsewhere in Tennessee, the county evidently was not a place African Americans wanted to live after the Civil War. When freedom came, both the formerly enslaved and the free blacks who had lived in the county before the war moved away. Today the black population hovers around 1 percent.[45]

I think about this absence of local blackness when I'm in a T-shirt store down the road from Dollywood on the Pigeon Forge Parkway. It sells a line of shirts from a company out of Georgia called Dixie Outfitters; its neo-Confederate wares sport slogans like "If this flag offends you, you need a history lesson."

Dixie Outfitters also sells a series of shirts that honor "Modern Day Southern Heritage Heros [*sic*]." One features Maurice Bessinger, whose restaurants once offered the most prominent examples of South Carolina–style barbecue.[46] Rather than try to catalog or bemoan the number of Confederate flags that can still be found in Pigeon Forge, I'd rather tell you about Bessinger and his Confederate barbecue.

Maurice's Piggie Park is in West Columbia, South Carolina, across the Congaree River from the state capital. *Park* suits the restaurant because it is actually small complex of buildings and sheds dedicated to the business of barbecuing. The site includes the restaurant, a smokehouse, a small office building, neon signs featuring pulled pork sandwiches, Bible quotes, and "Little Joe"—a smirking cartoon pig wearing a baseball cap. I felt a sense of anticipation as we approached—even a touch of nerves. It felt a little like we were witnessing a battlefield, a site not unlike Bunker Hill or Normandy, although *this* war is still raging.

Google "Maurice's BBQ" and you'll quickly find Bessinger's obits among the top results. They refer to him as a segregationist and an "unrepentant racist." Even if you've just been looking for an address, a chapter in the long racially divisive history of smoking pork will unfold on your web browser. In 1939 Maurice Bessinger's father opened a barbecue stand and taught his son the trade. From those humble beginnings young Maurice grew the roadside stand into one of the largest commercial barbecue operations in the United States by 1999.[47]

Throughout this explosive growth Bessinger adamantly situated himself on the wrong side of history. In the sixties he protested integration and joined the National Association for the Preservation of White People, an organization as deplorable as the name suggests. In 2000, when controversy reignited around the Confederate flag at the South Carolina State House, Maurice saw an opportunity to step into the limelight. At each of his fourteen restaurant locations, he proudly displayed large rebel flags and distributed tracts extolling the virtues of the plantation Confederacy and condemning the war crimes of Abraham Lincoln. The NAACP called for a boycott, and Bessinger lost millions as grocery stores and Walmart, and the US military canceled their standing orders for Maurice's bottled barbecue sauce.

When I visited West Columbia in February 2014, no Confederate flags were flying. The Piggie Park looked a little threadbare. The pavement was cracked and the parking lot awning was rusting. Weeds had sprung up around the office building, and at least one billboard has been simply painted white and left blank in the South Carolina sun. The tracts were gone, except for one tiny booklet from the Wordless Book Ministry of Seminole, Florida, explaining the lesson of John 3:16. The dark wood-paneled walls were mostly empty, covered in nails, and faded where Confederate propaganda once hung. I was expecting a battlefield; I found the site of a defeat.

Maurice Bessinger's son, Lloyd, took over the decaying business in October 2013 in an effort to save it from his father's Confederate partisanship. "Dad liked politics," he told Columbia's *The State,* "That's not something we're interested in doing. We want to serve great barbecue. We want to get past that."[48]

Since my visit things seem to be looking up. About two years after I went there, the *Charlotte Observer*'s food critic, Kathleen Purvis, ended a personal boycott of the Piggie Park, thanks to the rebel-ectomy. Her description sounds brighter than mine: "The atmosphere was friendly and down-home, a little like a Cracker Barrel. The barbecue, lightly smoky and moist, was a good example of the South Carolina style."[49] I suppose Maurice's Piggie Park is reluctantly edging toward progress. Perhaps one day I can love it in the way I love other old barbecue places: the signs, menus, and deep connection to their communities. In many ways, though, this is what made me uncomfortable about Maurice and his restaurant. It isn't *my* community. By stripping that place of its past, does it lose its character? Would I like the Piggie Park more if I didn't know its Confederate past? Probably. I don't know the politics of many of the pit masters who ran and run barbecue restaurants I have loved. Maybe we would have been copacetic, maybe not. I don't know if it is better not to know, but I do know that it is easier. The Bessingers clearly wanted to bury their father's politics with him, and they probably should be allowed to do just that. No sane person would begrudge them the opportunity to just serve barbecue and hold the politics. Right? Right.

Piggie Park serves fine barbecue. I had Bessinger's signature sandwich. The pork is cooked slowly over hickory wood, served with the mustard-based sauce that is the hallmark of Columbia and the Midlands. It was rich, tender, and smoky. The golden tangy sauce is attributed to

German immigrants who traveled down the Great Wagon Road from Pennsylvania and settled in the Midlands after arriving through the Port of Charleston in the mid-1800s. It is certainly possible that, with his Germanic surname, Maurice Bessinger's ancestors were among them. His version of the sauce is piquant with a touch of sweetness and a velvety texture. The sandwiches are served with chopped slaw and hush puppies, fried to a crisp crust with a delicate, moist interior. Our side order of onion rings was the real thing: fresh thick-sliced white onions that had been battered and deep-fried. They paired wonderfully with Maurice's Hickory Sauce.

When I went to Maurice's, a print near the men's restroom displayed the various flags of the generals of the Confederate States of America—the sole visible remnant of Maurice Bessinger's personal lost cause. We didn't know it at the time, but while we were eating our sandwiches, the eighty-three-year-old Bessinger was succumbing to Alzheimer's.[50] As we ate his family recipe, he breathed his last breath and left a world that had moved dramatically away from him. Today his battle is remembered on a sad misspelled shirt that retails for $14.99 at shitty souvenir stores in places like Pigeon Forge. They don't even sell it at his own restaurant. It's not always the winners who tell the story—losers sometimes write history too.

~

As early as the end of the nineteenth century, the idea of the mountain hillbilly was firmly implanted in American consciousness. These early incarnations were slightly different than the slack-jawed cartoon yokel I grew up watching, like *The Simpsons'* Cletus Spuckler or as portrayed in "Appalachian Emergency Room" on *Saturday Night Live*. In the early years the hillbilly was seen as a little purer, an Anglo-Saxon unsullied by modernity and profoundly in touch with the land around him (or her—though she didn't seem to get as much press). This lack of modernity, which for many mountain residents meant just that—lack—was seen as opportunity for preservation.

By the 1920s the National Park Service was keen to establish a major park in the East. The western parks, most notably Yellowstone and Yosemite, had been great successes, and the federal authorities wanted to try to stop the encroachment of eastern development.

Horace Kephart, a travel writer and librarian, describes "the dreamy blue haze of the [Smoky] mountains" as an almost spiritual force that "softens all outlines and lends a mirage-like effect of great distance to objects that are but a few miles off, while those farther removed grow more and more intangible until finally the sky-line blends with the sky itself."[51]

Kephart's eloquent depictions of the mountains and the life they contained were instrumental in boosting public support for the national park. Today his contributions are memorialized in the name of Mount Kephart, a six-thousand-foot peak on the border of Sevier County and North Carolina's Swain County.

Eventually, with the help of $5 million of Rockefeller money, the government secured a nucleus of land. However, there was still the matter of the people who happened to be residing on the land that was now going to be preserved.

One local legend tells of a family that the park service moved off their land. The family then settled in a valley not far away, only to be told again by the federal government that their home was going to be purchased for a new hydroelectric dam, to be built by the Tennessee Valley Authority. Finally, the family settled for a third time in Anderson County, Tennessee, not far from Knoxville. This time the Army Corps of Engineers kicked them out of their home, for the development of a community called Oak Ridge—home to the Manhattan Project. Out of luck three times in a row, the family gave up on Tennessee and moved to Kentucky, where their children and grandchildren happily remain.

Dolly's oldest sister, Willadeene, has written several memoirs detailing her family's history. In the first, *In the Shadow of a Song,* she tells of their great-grandparents, George and Cassie Ann Rayfield.[52] Both Rayfields were born in Sevier County around the time of the Civil War. After marrying in 1875, they lived in an area called Tater Ridge, about six miles from Gatlinburg in what is now known as the Greenbrier section of the national park.

Greenbrier was filled with Parton's ancestors. The first Parton to settle in the area was Benjamin Parton, a private in the Union cavalry.

Even today you can hike into the national park and see the Parton family cemetery. Hundreds of families like the Partons and the Rayfields had to be moved when the park was established.

The displacement was difficult, painful, and at times messy.[53] At times it must have seemed like a cataclysmic event, though now it feels like just a small step in the creation of the national park. That is how history works. The park has been a success, a place enjoyed by millions, and most regard the discomfort and hard feelings of those whom it displaced as small worthwhile sacrifice. In another generation that sacrifice may fall out of the narrative entirely.

Sometimes the homes, buildings, sheds, and other traces of life that the hundreds of displaced people left behind were removed as well. The park's administrators kept things that they felt would be representative of typical Appalachia. For example, they preserved a schoolhouse near where the Rayfields lived.[54] Another nearby example is the Walker Sisters' Home, which has become a popular destination for visiting tourists and hikers. The Walker sisters refused offers for relocation and declined to leave their land, despite multiple overtures from park officials. In what may be another local legend, President Franklin Delano Roosevelt is said to have personally attempted to convince the sisters to vacate the park.[55]

The sisters had agreed to sell their land to the park service only if they were granted a lifetime lease. The park service, which wasn't keen on the publicity that forcing five spinster sisters out of their homes would generate, allowed them to spend the remainder of their lives as a kind of living exhibit.

In 1946 the sisters were featured in the *Saturday Evening Post*. The reporter John Maloney wrote that the sisters had "kept any touch of these modern times away from their health, not through the slightest trace of eccentricity or any dislike of progress, but simply because, as women without menfolk around, they have continued doing things in the ways and with the implements they know best how to use—which is to say, their father's and grandfather's methods and tools."[56]

At first the national publicity led to some discomfort. Paul Gordon, the historian for the park, wrote in his 1975 application for recognition of the sisters' homestead as a national historic site that they weren't quite the typical Appalachians they were presented as being: "In actuality the sisters were as much of a relic in the mountains as if they had clung to ways outdated by 50 years in any other section of the country."[57]

The real reason the sisters chose to stay is anybody's guess—my inclination is that it was a far more deliberate choice than some notion that they couldn't find husbands. I think they saw the world changing and an entire lexicon of skill, traditions, and lore falling away, and they chose to hold on. It is not so different an impulse than Horace Kephart's desire to preserve the mountains themselves or the Pi Beta Phi sorority sisters' encouraging the residents of Gatlinburg to monetize local crafts rather than let them pass into obscurity.

Dolly Parton is acutely aware of these histories and traditions, first as a consumer. Dollywood employees, Parton's acquaintances, and Dollywood executives told me repeatedly that as a child and young performer in the 1950s, she learned about her home by experiencing the same kinds of attractions that outsiders did. It's unclear exactly what the young Parton saw, but it's easy to imagine that the displays of mountain craft in and around the national park and the hillbilly-themed attractions outside it were probably influential. Dollywood is part of a continuum of hospitality in Pigeon Forge. The theme park continues to operate what it calls legacy attractions, key features that are deemed distinct signifiers of mountain life. These attractions, some of which were present when the young Parton visited Gold Rush Junction as a guest, serve as signifiers of not only mountain life but the history of marketing that image. The very idea of legacy attractions speaks to expectations. Could Dollywood claim to represent mountain life without including crafts? Likewise, a train rolling through the wooded terrain of the Smokies serves as a symbol that Dollywood is an Appalachian park. These essential ingredients tell people that they are in the mountains and give the distinct impression that it would be impossible for Dollywood to exist anywhere else.

Appalachia's financial struggles stem from a history of extractive industries' entering the mountain South in the late nineteenth and early twentieth centuries. This exploitation has created a rather famous downtrodden working-class population. The continuation of this pattern of poverty created a class eager for other economic opportunities, including the hospitality industry. As road trips became the de rigueur vacation for the middle class after World War II, working-class residents in the mountains found hosting tourists was in many ways preferable to tenant farming, logging, or mining. The theme parks, hotels, and attractions were safe and relatively easy places to earn a living, compared to digging coal, even if the wages tended to be lower.

Portrayals of the imagined romantic mountains soon slipped into stereotypes. C. Brenden Martin writes that the image of poor mountaineers who loved moonshine and were quick to feud was a popular trope by the early years of the twentieth century: "As Americans increasingly regarded the southern highlands as a backward region inhabited by a poverty-stricken and depraved people, a new derogatory term was coined to describe mountain residents—hillbilly."[58]

The Dollywood replica of Dolly Parton's childhood home. *Photo by author*

Sign outside the replicated cabin. *Photo by author*

The DreamMore Resort, Pigeon Forge. *Photo by author*

Dolly keeps an eye on the Pigeon Forge Parkway. *Photo by author*

Cas Walker's Super Market, Dollywood. *Photo by author*

Robert F. Thomas Chapel in Dollywood, named for the doctor who delivered Dolly Parton. *Photo by author*

The Dollywood Express. *Photo by author*

Hillbillies for sale, Pigeon Forge. *Photo by author*

Hill-Billy Village, once one of the oldest attractions on the Pigeon Forge Parkway, now defunct. *Photo by author*

Downtown Gatlinburg. *Photo by author*

Moonshine for sale at The Island, Pigeon Forge. *Photo by author*

The Coat of Many Colors display, Dollywood. *Photo by author*

It's Dolly's world, we're just visitors, Dollywood. *Photo by author*

Dollywood, Pigeon Forge. *Photo by author*

Daisy Mae, Dreams, and Dolly

They portray mountain people [as if] we are all these dumb barefoot hillbillies. I think country people are the smartest people in the world, and I've been everywhere.

—Dolly Parton[1]

"DOLLY, WHERE I come from would I have called you a hillbilly?" asked Barbara Walters in 1977. "If you had, it would have probably been very natural, but I'd have probably kicked your shins," Parton replied. She continued, "We're the ones you would consider the *Li'l Abner* people, Daisy Mae, and that sort of thing—they took that from people like us. But, we're a very proud people. People with class—it was country class, but it was a great deal of class."[2]

Stereotypes are a complicated thing. Sure, they invite oversimplification and reduction. Confusing them with an actual understanding of another culture is a toxic mistake, but stereotypes are also incredibly effective brands. Parton seems to understand that her upbringing, her origin story, sends a signal to the rest of the word that says hillbilly. That association seems to endear her to people who share that background and creates an unmistakable air of authenticity for those who don't.

You know exactly what a hillbilly is supposed to look like. They are always white and usually bearded and barefoot. Hillbillies like to sing and hate to work. The mountain stereotype tends to have one of two faces: dim-witted and lazy but harmless—too stupid to damage anyone but himself—or violent, drunken louts who are incapable of controlling their sexual urges. Fueled by moonshine, the hillbilly is likely to fire a blunderbuss to scare off outsiders and/or is prone to try to have sex with anything that moves (including blood relatives and livestock). Overalls and a big floppy straw hat are, of course, the outfit of choice.

Hillbilly women get a similar treatment. Whether they are shown as unhealthy and ragged or loose, fertile, and lethargic, the hillbilly archetype isn't particularly flattering for the ladies, either. Hillbilly women are the target of not only derision but also lust. Buxom and usually blonde in this incarnation, the hillbilly women are usually depicted as man crazy, horny, and just as dim as their male counterparts. A favorite trope of hillbilly comics and cartoons is a voluptuous bride, or her father, marching to the church with a hapless boyfriend at gunpoint—the birth of the shotgun wedding.

Popular culture sees Dolly Parton tying her future to this version of the caricature. Blonde, buxom, and beautiful, she was like a country music version of *Li'l Abner*'s Daisy Mae come to life.

Daisy Mae is as responsible as any character for the popular notion of a hillbilly vixen. The cartoonist Al Capp created her in 1934 as a romantic foil for his good-natured but dim-witted hero, Li'l Abner. Love-struck, Daisy chased Abner all over their fictional hometown of Dogpatch, Kentucky. Daisy wasn't any smarter than Abner, but she wasn't quite as lazy—she had a man to catch. Her scant outfit has become something of a trope in and of itself: a polka-dot peasant top and a short skirt torn at the hem are often used as shorthand for a hillbilly pinup. In fact, Parton posed in just such an outfit on a hay bale for a 1978 poster.

Daisy Mae must have had some resonance with Parton. In 1989's "White Limozeen" she sang of a heroine who sounds more than a little like Parton herself. Parton describes the "hometown girl" with "eyes full of stars [and] a heart full of dreams" who comes to the big city seeking stardom as "Daisy Mae in Hollywood."[3]

In the early years of her career Parton played a bit at being the hometown girl with starry eyes. It seems hard to imagine now, but in early interviews with national figures like Johnny Carson or in the Walters interview, Parton seems earnest, bashful, and sometimes even a little embarrassed but—and this is important—never *ever* outmatched. Parton uses her hillbilly background as a tool. She bends the stereotype in the direction that suits her. We already know that, culturally speaking, a hillbilly is connected to the environment, is poor, and has a genuine personality. All Parton had to do was strip away the negatives. Her brilliance proves that she is not stupid, and her effervescent personality proves she's not lazy.

Her life story is the stuff of country music legend: Parton was born in a one-room cabin and delivered by a doctor who was paid with a sack of cornmeal. She was one of twelve children and her parents were sharecroppers. She jokes that when she was a child her family was so poor that "the ants used to bring back food they'd taken from us because they felt sorry for us."[4] When Parton was growing up, her family had to do without electricity and indoor plumbing. These facts appear in Parton's biography, in large part, I think, because we want—no, we *need*—our country stars to have biographies that ring true to the genre. Dolly Parton's biography rings as true as any. To paraphrase David Allan Coe's song: if Dolly Parton ain't country, I'll kiss your ass.[5]

The historian Bill Malone describes her as a member of "the last generation of performers who really had direct working-class roots or who could recall rural experiences" and adds that successive generations "have been increasingly region-less, classless, and suburban in residence and values."[6] Parton is a link to a kind of country music that barely exists anymore. What separates Parton from the other members of this 'last generation is that, unlike Loretta Lynn, Merle Haggard, Buck Owens, or Willie Nelson, she was born after World War II. Her

Appalachian roots carry a legacy of the Depression-era ethos associated with country artists a generation older than she.

We do in fact associate a certain kind of upbringing or coming-of-age, usually Depression era, with the greatest generation of performers. Haggard, Owens, Lynn, and Nelson were born during the Depression. Bill Monroe and Ernest Tubb formed their first bands and Hank Williams learned to play guitar during that time. But Dolly Parton was born seven years after the Depression ended. She seems to be from that older era because the Depression came early to many mountain communities and has never left. Fusing Depression-era ideas about poverty with geography creates an easy (if lazy) shorthand that demands an impoverished background of people who come from Appalachia.

There was, and still is, a great deal of poverty in Appalachia. For many outsiders this has become a defining characteristic, but even this is not universally true. There are rich Appalachians and educated ones. Appalachia has plenty of driven people. My point here is that, like any huge geographic and cultural region, all kinds of things are happening in the mountains. Nothing about the hillbilly image is necessarily true—except, of course, that it seems to sell really well.

Almost as soon as the term became popularized, it became a selling point. Ten years before Al Capp introduced readers to Daisy Mae and the other residents of Dogpatch, Ralph Peer was marketing southern white pop music as "hillbilly records." Seminal early country artists like Jimmie Rodgers and the Carter Family recorded for Peer as hillbilly artists.[7] Hillbilly as a genre hung around until the fifties. When the white kids started getting into rhythm and blues they became a new kind of billy—a rockabilly. Some of the rockabillies split their loyalties between rock and country for a while—think of Elvis or Jerry Lee Lewis, who both toyed with country from time to time. For the most part, though, the "rock" greatly outweighed the "billy," and that genre moved further and further away from its hillbilly roots.

In Nashville, hillbilly fell out of favor for the more respectable-sounding "country music." In 1958 a collection of Nashville executives formed the Country Music Association, which sought to elevate the genre.[8] "Country and western," and eventually just "country," became the favored nomenclature. Nashville performers moved away from farm-inspired attire and toward western-style clothing and hats. Hillbillies were once again relegated to the mountains.

In a 2014 interview with *Southern Living,* Parton shared what she thinks of when she hears the term *hillbilly*: "To me that's not an insult. We were just mountain people. We were really redneck, roughneck, hillbilly people. And I'm proud of it." She expanded on the kinds of terms that get thrown at people from the mountains: "'White trash!' I am. People always say 'Aren't you insulted when people call you white trash?' I say, 'Well it depends on who's calling me white trash and how they mean it.' But we really were to some degree. Because when you're that poor and you're not educated, you fall in those categories. But I'm proud of my hillbilly, white trash background. To me that keeps you humble; that keeps you good. And it doesn't matter how hard you try to outrun it—if that's who you are, that's who you are. It'll show up once in a while."[9]

In reading interviews of Dolly, you quickly begin to realize how masterful she can be at directing the conversation. Many of the one-liners are well honed, repeated on many different talk shows and in interviews. Dolly Parton reveals quite a bit about herself in these comedic bits, but she never reveals more than she intends. Parton's lines give just enough information about her hardscrabble upbringing: "We didn't have any electricity except for the lightning bugs. If fireflies were out, we'd catch them in a mason jar and put them in our bedroom! We did have running water . . . we would *run* and get it. [*laughs*] Most people have four rooms and a bath; we had one room and a *path*. We had the little outdoor shack out back. It was a good life, and I loved growing up in the mountains. We were really just people, and God and family meant everything to us."[10]

A line she is fond of using, particularly when she's on stage, involves her eleven siblings: "My parents weren't Catholic, they were just horny hillbillies!"[11] These kinds of jokes work for her in a way that they might not for Snuffy Smith or a hillbilly in a Bugs Bunny cartoon. First, the line confirms that Parton is a hillbilly and that her music and her persona are not a put-on—they are authentic. We recognize from pop culture that hillbillies are *supposed* to be horny, so when it is confirmed for us, it rings true. That Dolly Parton says it rather than Cuzin Clem or Li'l Abner complicates things. We know that Dolly isn't a buffoon. Even someone with a cursory knowledge of her career knows that she has been tremendously savvy and successful—she's brilliant. So Dolly Parton—nobody's dumb hillbilly—waves at the stereotype while keeping her distance.

The historian Patrick Huber examines the sociohistoric implications of hillbilly souvenirs. He argues that the upheaval of racial norms during the civil rights movement of the 1960s required those who had previously relied on racial stereotypes to market and define the South to look for more innocuous alternatives.[12] The hillbilly became a recognizable icon for white tourists that was less offensive to post-1960s sensibilities than the African American stereotypes that had dominated southern tourist souvenirs in the first half of the twentieth century and before.

Hillbilly imagery has proved to be remarkably resilient. Even into the twenty-first century the hillbilly remains a figure on which Americans can project feelings of regional and class superiority. The rise of redneck reality TV—shows like *Hollywood Hillbillies, Duck Dynasty, Moonshiners,* and *Hillbilly Hand Fishing*—reflects commercial media's continued tolerance for the trope.

Similarly, hillbilly-themed parties remain persistently popular on college campuses. Young women don overalls, blacken their teeth, and go barefoot. Male students accessorize with long fake beards or straw hats, while the women wear curlers in their hair and stuff pillows in their tops to look pregnant while darkening an eye to suggest abuse. They wave Confederate flags. Sometimes these are called "white trash parties," but the intent seems to be the same.

In fact, the conflation of white trash and hillbilly is an intersection worth some examination. The terms are, in the most significant ways, synonyms. Both connote a poor person who lives with little access to, and even less regard for, the rest of society. Both terms refer to somebody so clueless about civilized life that they live on the razor's edge of attraction and repulsion. It is fun to play white trash, but fun made only by the ability to stop being white trash.

While popular images of the hillbilly are implicitly racial—a black hillbilly generally isn't part of the vernacular—and white trash is, obviously, an explicitly racial term. The phrase is probably at least as old as *hillbilly*; its origins date at least to the antebellum South. In 1854 Harriet Beecher Stowe used the phrase extensively in her *Key to Uncle Tom's Cabin,* the sequel to her famous novel and rebuttal to Southern claims that she had neglected the so-called benevolent aspects of chattel slavery.[13]

White trash is a term rooted in notions of white supremacy; someone who is white trash has forfeited the supposedly innate superiority granted them by virtue of their whiteness. They should, this line of reasoning goes, be at the apex of the racial ladder, but their poverty and lack of sophistication keep them in the underclass.[14]

Although the term is deeply rooted in both nineteenth-century slang and prejudice, *white trash* has proved to have some real staying power. Remarkably, *white trash* seems to be more a pernicious term in public discourse than *hillbilly,* as evidenced by those white trash costumes and themed events.

In 2012 a health care lobbying firm held a white trash–themed networking event on Capitol Hill.[15] The White Trash Bash is a staple on college campuses, and white trash and hillbilly costumes abound in costume shops and Halloween stores. One party-planning website, The College Party Guru, offers this summary of such parties: "Celebrate the South, trailer parks and Wal-Mart parking lots. Don't worry about being trashy; grow out that mullet and start stocking up on Bush [*sic*] Light beer because it [*sic*] time to throw a White Trash party!"[16]

Like blackface, a white trash costume gives someone who already enjoys a degree of social flexibility a license to bend the rules of convention. When these images of hillbillies are played for humor, they tend to be nonthreatening and relatively benign, but they are almost always condescending.

Hillbillies are tied to a place. They reside in a specific set of hills—the mountain South. White trash, on the other hand, is placeless—it might refer to a hillbilly, but it might also refer to any number of lower-income groups of whites (Oklahoma's Okies and Florida's crackers come to mind). The homeland of the popular hillbilly is really two separate regions, which are often lumped together (as I just did) as "the mountain South." In fact, about six hundred miles and the

Mississippi River separate Appalachia and the Ozarks. For example, the characters of *The Beverly Hillbillies* (1962) are usually depicted as moving to California from the Ozarks, but Daisy Moses (known as Granny by all) sometimes refers to her home in Limestone, which is near Johnson City, Tennessee—firmly Appalachian territory. But none of this seems to matter to people who are eager to buy in to the image or to sell it. After all, if someone in Appalachian Pigeon Forge wants to sell something with an Ozark character on it, are they making fun of themselves or the folks to the west—or are they just trying to make some money?

These cultural displays create expectations in outsiders who associate the southern mountains with hillbilly life. The popularity of cartoons like *Li'l Abner* and *Snuffy Smith* in the 1930s and 1940s led to a midcentury cultural hillbilly boom.[17] Americans eagerly consumed baby boomer situation comedies filled with southern "home-grown hijinks" and innocent spectacle, like *The Beverly Hillbillies*. Others came along too: *Petticoat Junction* in 1963 and the variety show *Hee Haw* in 1969. This cultural saturation led to a desire to see the real thing, and entrepreneurs in the mountains were more than happy to oblige. Attractions like hillbilly miniature golf, souvenir stores, and country dinner shows appeared near the entrance to the Great Smoky Mountains National Park. Tourists were delighted with the displays they found in Sevier County, which were largely constructed not out of local custom or necessity but to meet the expectation of outsiders. Instead of pickin' or shinin', tourism had become the authentic local tradition.

~

When Parton expresses frustration with the hillbilly image, she might be talking about the thin simplifications and goofy characters on *Hee Haw*, but I'm sure it is the darker side to that mountain image that bothered her the most. A popular idea that is much harder to find represented in Pigeon Forge gift shops but that runs rampant throughout national popular culture is the notion of the mountains as a brutal, uncivil, and violent place—a place where the population is so uneducated and disconnected that no act of brutality is beyond them. These are the violent, monstrous hillbillies of the 1972 film *Deliverance* or the TV series *Justified*, which ran from 2010 to 2015. This version of the trope uses hillbillies as figures who aren't really people. The natural landscape of the mountains becomes a place where anything can happen and the people who live there are capable of the worst kinds of savagery. In this version violence and poverty are congenital—these people are a different breed, one that fails in the rest of the country. They cannot and will not be civilized. This image, more than any other, is one that Dollywood contradicts. But it is also an image that extends far beyond the world of entertainment.

Here's an idea of what Parton was up against: in 1974 the author Nathaniel Weyl, a eugenics proponent, wrote a paper with the discourteous title "The Geography of Stupidity in the U.S.A."[18] In it he attempts to chart the regions of the United States that are most lacking in intelligence by looking at the failure rate of white applicants on the Armed Forces Qualification Test in 1968. Kentucky, Tennessee, and West Virginia did the worst. Weyl writes that these low test scores are caused by the "mental defectives" from Appalachia. The region, he helpfully explains, without citing any sources, was settled by "deported English felons and paupers, of the scourings of the poorhouses, of those sent to America because brain damage or innate low intelligence made it impossible for them to earn a livelihood at home."[19]

As faulty and unappealing as Weyl is as a researcher and scholar, it is worth noting that the general particulars of his narrative probably are not unfamiliar to anyone from the mountains. The idea that hillbillies are somehow from inferior stock is an old one. The arguments are weak and spurious at best, stupid and spiteful at worst—but that doesn't mean that they don't cut deep in a region that struggles with issues much more real than eugenic philosophy.

You can still find similar sentiments without looking too hard. In a 2009 episode of *The O'Reilly Factor* the Fox News host Bill O'Reilly echoed Weyl's argument, saying, "The culture in Appalachia harms the children almost beyond repair." He went on to explain that the people who live in the mountains deserve whatever tough breaks they may have received because they aren't smart enough, or motivated enough, to leave. "If I'm born in Appalachia the first chance I get—I go to Miami," O'Reilly declared. "Because that's where the jobs are, but they stay there in the cycle of poverty for two hundred years."[20] It is telling that O'Reilly said these things in an effort to argue the hopelessness of Diane Sawyer's efforts to encourage investment in Appalachia. O'Reilly, like Weyl, was arguing against helping the region because the people there, in his view, are simply not people worth saving. Hillbillies are less than people. His most telling pronouncement came near the end of the segment: "I don't want to rebuild the infrastructure of Appalachia. I want to leave it pristine. It's beautiful."[21] It is an argument that echoes through the history of this place, an argument that says, Why fix poverty when it can be used as local color? It's the same argument that winds its way through Detroit's "Ruin Porn" (defined by a contributor to CNN.com as "the work of photographers and artists who aim to communicate the romantic frisson—as they see it—of run-down buildings") or the colorful postcards of Caribbean slums.[22] Dolly Parton certainly doesn't believe her people aren't worth saving. She may have left, but she never stops coming back and never stops pushing back against the weight of collective low expectations.

∼

I'm arguing that Dollywood is a corrective for the stereotypes that have annoyed the population in Appalachia for more than a century. Yet Dollywood's staff has plenty of men with beards who wear overalls and ladies in bonnets. Dolly Parton makes jokes about being a hillbilly—just a few paragraphs ago I quoted her as saying her family is white trash. So does Parton do any damage if she confirms mountain stereotypes? I find it hard to imagine that she does. Parton is so relentlessly positive, and beloved by so many groups of people, that it seems that her proudly waving a hillbilly banner bends the stereotype in a positive direction.

In 2006 a slightly sinister-sounding company called Omnicom developed a survey that, the firm claimed, could track the general public's awareness of celebrities. The survey added a new dimension to the decades-old Q-Rating, which reflects the public's knowledge of a celebrity, a company, a brand, and the like and whether the public likes the person or thing in question. The Davie-Brown Index, or DBI, was developed for advertisers seeking celebrity endorsements. It takes on the impossible-sounding task of quantifying perception. Put simply, the DBI attempts to rank the degree to which people deem a famous person trustworthy.[23] It probably shouldn't come as a surprise that Parton ranks as the best-known country performer and has consistently ranked among the top ten most–trusted celebrities.[24] Parton didn't get where she is by rubbing people the wrong way. That shy but direct young performer whom Barbara Walters interviewed in the 1970s didn't tell people who *they* were, she told them who *she* was. I've watched and read a lot of what Parton has had to say over the years, and I think that's an important distinction. She never makes fun of her audience or her hometown; she'd rather speak about how proud she is to be a Tennessean or an Appalachian or a hillbilly—whichever. If Parton calls herself "white trash," perhaps it takes the sting out of the term for people who have heard it thrown their way at work or at school. If the amazing and incredible Dolly Parton is white trash, then why wouldn't you want to be too?

Parton understands how helpful that kind influence can be, because she has been on the rough end of teasing and taunting. Today Parton has become a remarkable booster of education all over the world. Her philanthropy has created real opportunities for school kids, particularly in her hometown. But it seems that when she was attending those same schools, she didn't always love the experience.

Going to school can be rough for anybody. If you are different, it's even worse, and if that difference is how much money your family has, then the world can feel pretty cold. In her autobiography, *Dolly,* Parton describes struggling with the reality of her family's poverty. She recalls students' being asked what they had eaten for breakfast, and reports, "I became more and more embarrassed about the fact that all we ever ate for breakfast was biscuits and gravy. Other kids were recalling glorious breakfasts of eggs, sausage, bacon, orange juice, and all kinds of things that seemed wonderful and luxurious. I hated my biscuits and gravy. I wanted to gag them up and poverty along with them."[25]

Parton recounts many such instances of leaving a home without electricity or running water and going to school, where she and her siblings were subjected to the taunts and jibes of classmates. Perhaps the most famous of these stories is recounted in one of her best-loved songs. In "Coat of Many Colors," Parton tells of a coat her mother made for her, sewn of "rags of many colors." She sings about how her mother made the coat with love, telling a young Dolly the Bible story of Joseph and his coat of many colors. Parton was thrilled with the care her mother took to make the coat and couldn't wait to show it off. She was shocked when she got to school and the other children began to sneer at her. "Soon it turned into a whole room full of mocking faces; laughing, pointing, jeering at me . . . me and my coat. I wanted to tell them the story Mama had told about Joseph and make them understand how special, how singular, how beautiful . . . but they would not hear it."[26]

Parton told *Rolling Stone*'s Chet Flippo that the cruelty was scarring, "a very sad and cutting memory that I long kept deep within myself. . . . I didn't have a blouse on under [the coat] because I had done *well* just to have a jacket to wear. So when the kids kept sayin' I didn't have a shirt on under it, I said I *did* because I was embarrassed. So they broke the buttons off my coat. They locked me in the coat closet that day and held the door closed and it was black dark in there and I just went into a screaming fit. I remembered that and I was ashamed to even mention it, and for *years* I held it in my mind."[27]

In 2015 Parton partnered with NBC to produce a series of TV movies based on her life and songs.[28] The first, *Coat of Many Colors,* premiered that December. The film begins with Parton sitting on a sleigh in front of Dollywood's Showstreet Palace Theater, which is decorated for Christmas. "Oh, don't you think my home looks beautiful?" she says as she greets viewers. "I'm so proud of my theme park here in the Great Smoky Mountains of East Tennessee." She introduces the film by saying, "My favorite song that I've ever written tells a true story from my childhood about a little coat that my mama made for me. Of course, she called it my 'Coat of Many Colors.'"[29]

The movie spins the legend of young Dolly's coat a little further than we've ever heard before. In the movie version, like the song, her mother sews her the coat while telling Dolly the story of Joseph. As she told Flippo, the other school kids cruelly strip her and lock her in a closet. And as in her autobiography, the young Dolly learns through the experience the value of resilience.

The movie strengthens the story's relationship to the biblical parable. It also ties the crafting of the coat and Parton's recovery from the subsequent assault and the family's grief at the death of Parton's infant brother, Larry.

The other new layer that the movie adds to the story is Judy Ogle, Parton's longtime companion and personal assistant. The film introduces Ogle as Parton's personal savior—she uses a Tennessee state flag to single-handedly beat back the bullies who have trapped Parton.

In her autobiography Parton doesn't mention anything quite so dramatic about when she first met Ogle. Instead she recalls that they met in the third grade when Parton transferred schools. Young Parton was fascinated with Ogle's bright red hair. The two "fish out of water" formed a friendship and "made a great pair."[30] The two remain close today, and by all accounts Ogle still is a central part of Parton's entourage and Parton's closest confidante.

Coat of Many Colors ends with the young Parton's religious reawakening, and Parton sings her famous composition as a voiceover.

In the song Parton finds this memory as if by accident: "I go wanderin' once again" to "the seasons of my youth." It is wistful, melancholy, sad, and warm all at once. Parton considers it her finest work as a songwriter.[31] That coat is on display in a small glass case at Dollywood now. It is worn by a mannequin made of fallen autumn leaves and is next to a notebook in which Parton has handwritten the lyrics. On the wall behind the case is an enlarged photo of a group of children, who sneer, point, and laugh at the viewer.

∼

When work is hard to come by or money is scarce, finding things to be proud of can be difficult. A big part of why the hillbilly archetype cuts so deeply through our culture is poverty. It tacitly excuses the lack of opportunities some people face. Someone born poor in a downtrodden community will have a harder time achieving success than if they had been born in a financially more advantageous locale. Many popular images of Appalachia excuse this disparity. They tell us that hillbillies are poor because they are lazy, they live in ramshackle homes because they like to be close to nature, and they are uneducated because book learning doesn't make any difference in their world.

The caricature tries to wash away the complex nature of poverty with the same old pull-yourself-up-by-your-bootstraps fantasy that has coursed through American thought for generations. Hillbillies are part of an entire system of stereotypes that is used in place of empathy for impoverished people. Like welfare queens or shiftless immigrants, the hillbilly is a block against the knotty economic and social realities that might challenge our rhetoric about self-reliance. After all, how's a bare-foot bumpkin supposed to pull up his bootstraps?

The hillbilly is a complicated thing. How can the hillbilly be at once a load of crap, a (mildly) subversive icon, and an assertion of identity? Because we *need* stereotypes, and not just to pigeonhole other people: we need them to construct our own identities too.

Mark A. Roberts is a scholar and author who has written extensively about the cultural impact of hillbillies within Appalachia. He also knows Dollywood. In fact he claims Granny Ogle—of Dollywood's Granny Ogle's Ham 'n' Beans Restaurant—as a relative. So he knows whereof he speaks when he writes that Dollywood allows Appalachian visitors to "pay reverence" to their history. He continues, "Many Dollywood visitors gain a sense of their cultural selves from their tourist experiences."[32]

In his master's thesis Roberts tells a story about a group of sisters in West Virginia who take him to see their family homestead. His description of the trip is a perfect realization of an imagined hillbilly landscape: He travels by four-wheeler through woods and over hill and holler to get to a family clearing. There are stories about moonshiners. There is fiddle and banjo music. But out on the porch things get really interesting, because the family has built a wooden stage for performances and modeled it after a certain somebody's theme park.

> The hand-painted signs directing family and visitors to various parts of the homestead, the music stage set up specifically to be viewed from the front porch of the house, the image of the hillbilly finely illustrated on the side of an abandoned trailer—all these details created a place that felt like an amusement park:

it resembled Dollywood's simulated makeshift structures, its music stages designed to appear rustic, its repeated depiction of hillbillies. But the Muncy homestead was *real,* or was it a simulation?[33]

I think the answer is both. Dollywood is real. Like the old oxymoron, it actually is an authentic reproduction. The park is modeled after some real culture, sure. But certainly at least some of what today is sold as hillbilly culture or mountain culture evolved from a desire to entertain the tourists who have tramped their way through the mountains for more than a century now. Elements of the stereotype are true. Poverty, for example, is obviously a very real thing. That reality makes it possible to manufacture the cartoon of the broke mountaineer. As Dolly proves, shaping your culture into an image that pleases visitors was (and is) a lucrative maneuver. The glassblowers and leather crafters may well have deep historical antecedents in the hills, but they also owe a debt to Barnum and Disney.

The hillbilly makes Dollywood both possible and interesting. Without the commercial idea of the hillbilly, the businessmen who built the original park would have been far less likely to see Appalachia as a sound investment. Without Dolly Parton and her tacit critique of the depiction of hillbillies, the park would be just another cluster of roller coasters on the map of American tourist traps.

The train at Dollywood, the Dollywood Express (formerly the Rebel Railroad), in use since 1961, is built on a narrow-gauge railway, which echoes the railroads built in the mountains for the logging and coal industries.[34] Craftsman's Valley, which offers visitors an opportunity to observe and interact with traditional craftspeople, is not unlike the artisans about whom Allen Eaton writes in *Handicrafts of the Southern Highlands* (1937).[35]

Eaton was a champion of Appalachian artisans and their crafts. He worked in the mountains during the Depression and encouraged the cultivation and celebration of artisanal goods.[36] He went on to found the still-active Southern Highland Handicraft Guild, and wrote that craft makers developed a "hope of creation" and "the self-respect that comes with usefulness." He felt that these goods could be a kind of lifeline for the region, because "they offer the only means by which to earn money to pay taxes and buy the few necessities required to support a tolerable standard of life."[37]

Eaton's work, along with that of the craft-focused settlement schools, led to an understanding of the financial and cultural usefulness of folk arts that is still very present in Pigeon Forge and at Dollywood in particular. They have come to function like so many other attractions in the area: people expect crafts, and their expectations are met with glee.

The selection of crafts at Dollywood has become enormous. What was originally a single blacksmith's shop in Rebel Railroad's Confederate Village now includes wood-carvers, glassblowers, sign painters, wheelwrights, leather workers, candle makers, and millers. Parton's management partners, the Ozark-based Herschend Family Entertainment, added many of these crafts when they owned the park, which they called Silver Dollar City, after their successful theme park in Missouri. It operated under that name until 1986 when the park reopened as Dollywood.[38] Prior to Dolly's involvement, the Herschends, who bought the park in 1976, had wanted to bring visitors closer to mountain life by demonstrating local craft traditions—a practice that dates to the very earliest sites of Smoky Mountain tourism. Handicrafts have been strongly tied to tourism in the mountains for generations and especially since the handicraft revival of the early twentieth century.[39] This revival was led in large part by the settlement schools, a social reform movement that attempted to create an Appalachian culture based on the small-scale crafting of easily marketable goods like baskets and pottery.

In the early 1950s the Herschend family moved from Chicago to Branson, Missouri. The family enjoyed vacationing in the Ozarks and the patriarch, Hugo Herschend, secured a lease on the local attraction, Marvel Cave. Before Hugo could enjoy his new purchase, he died unexpectedly of a heart attack in 1955, leaving his wife, Mary, and son, Jack, who was fresh out of the Marines, to manage the cave. As part of a series of renovations Jack opened an above-ground attraction, Silver Dollar City, in 1960.[40]

A year later Jack's brother, Pete, began marketing the mountain theme park with TV tie-ins: "He invited the stars of the hit comedy Car

54, Where Are You? to manage opening-day crowds in 1963 and introduced a craft fair in the fall, typically a slow time. Shooting five episodes of The Beverly Hillbillies on location in 1967 sealed Silver Dollar City's popularity: Attendance rose 16 percent the next year to 900,000 visitors."[41]

Having cornered the market in Branson, the Herschends looked to expand. They found Goldrush Junction in Pigeon Forge; it was attracting tourists but losing money.[42] In 1976 the brothers purchased the ailing park and rebuilt it as a twin of their Branson theme park. Many attractions from this period remain in some form today, most notably the artisans.

In the early 1980s Dolly Parton made it known that she was interested in establishing a theme park near her hometown. Jack Herschend saw an opportunity, and, rather than compete with Parton, the Herschends offered her a piece of their park. That deal made Parton part owner, changed the name to Dollywood, and gave Parton creative control. "They are great Christian people and the best theme park operators in the industry," she said of her partners.[43] The success of this partnership has made both Parton and the Herschends a great deal of money. While Parton remains the sole visible owner of Dollywood (many incorrectly assume that she built the park and owns it outright), the Herschends continue to be nearly silent partners.

The Herschends are the managers of the park. Parton has little to do with the day-to-day management. "I don't even want to know about that," she said. "The success of both Dollywood and Dixie Stampede comes from our ability to each work in the areas of our expertise. Because believe me, if I were in charge of the daily operation, I know I would give away far too many tickets and, certainly, colas and ice cream to all the kids!"[44]

The Herschends manage three amusement parks and three water parks. They also either manage or own outright several dinner theaters (including the Dixie Stampede), showboats, sightseeing companies, and the attractions at Stone Mountain, Georgia. The Herschends are no longer just experts in selling the mountains or even the South; in 2013 the Herschends became the owners of the famed Harlem Globetrotters basketball team, giving the family one the most idiosyncratic portfolios in business.

Parton joined forces with the Herschends because she wanted an attraction unlike any that had ever been, a Disneyland for the mountain South. "I've always joked that I want to be a female Walt Disney," Parton has said. "In my early days, I thought if I do get successful, I want to come back here and build something special to honor my parents and my people."[45] She did not want Dollywood to be just roller coasters and stereotypes: "I've always been aggravated about how they portray mountain people in Hollywood."[46] Parton wanted mountain tourists to see what mountain life was all about and to celebrate instrument makers, blacksmiths, weavers, glassblowers, wood-carvers, potters, and leather workers. The Parton biographer Stephen Miller describes the folkloric work done by Dollywood's crafts people: "Dollywood has subsequently pursued a policy of research, sometimes with the use of scouts, to find people who still possess these traditional skills and find a place for them. In this way the park has helped to maintain and pre-serve crafts which might otherwise have died out."[47]

⌒

Dollywood is not separate from this history of a constructed narrative of Appalachia. It is very much part of it. While for many Parton was nothing more than a physical embodiment of Daisy Mae Scragg, in life Parton has proved to be so much more. She played to this image onstage but played against type off-stage, proving herself one of American music's savviest businesswomen, a generous philanthropist, and a leading advocate of the region. Now that region, *her* region, is home to Dollywood, the only amusement park in the world dedicated to a woman's life and history.[48]

Drawing a straight line from Pi Beta Phi's settlement school, Arrowmont, in Gatlinburg to Dolly Parton's Craftsman's Valley probably is not totally accurate, but there are shared impulses. The women of Arrowmont shared with Parton an impulse toward cultural preservation and a dedication to education (the Pi Beta Phis also founded Gatlinburg's first public school). Bill O'Reilly's opinions aside, they also shared an interest in providing the region with the tools to be successful. Arrowmont has followed Allen Eaton's model and fostered the craftwork of local artisans. Parton has, in characteristic fashion, gone big with her support of the county. In addition to her work with schoolchildren, she has initiated programs to encourage high school graduation, created a youth literacy program, donated thousands to Sevier County schools, and rebuilt the local hospital—including a $100,000 donation to the birthing unit. This meant that locals would no longer have to drive to Knoxville to have their babies.[49]

On November 23, 2016, a fire was sighted in Great Smoky Mountains National Park. At that time the fire was about the size of a football field. Because of a historic drought and a series of unpredictable winds, the fire quickly grew out of control. It consumed acre after acre in the park and then tore through Sevier County. Hamstrung by power outages and downed cell service, efforts to evacuate Gatlinburg were left to first responders who had to go door to door to clear homes in the blaze's path. In the end the fire consumed more than seventeen thousand acres, destroyed or damaged 2,460 buildings, and killed fourteen people.[50] Hundreds of Sevier County residents were rendered homeless. Because they evacuated so quickly, many were unable to save even basic necessities from their homes.

With her home county devastated, Parton stepped in to help. What might have been surprising to some was the extent of her generosity. Before she had raised a cent of outside funds, she promised to provide each family that lost a home $1,000 a month. She called the project the My People Fund, which borrows its name from a show at Dollywood that features members of the Parton family.

Then Parton asked for help. Lodge, a venerable East Tennessee cast-iron manufacturer, made a special skillet and gave $15 from each sale to Dolly's foundation. The skillets sold out in four and a half hours. Lodge rearranged its production schedule to make more, which also sold out quickly. In about ten days the skillets raised about $100,000. Parton also broadcast a telethon featuring performers like Kenny Rogers, Chris Stapleton, and Reba McEntire. Others called in to give donations. Paul Simon gave $100,000 and so did Taylor Swift. All told,

Parton's broadcast raised more than $9 million.[51] During the telethon Parton showed clips of some people who had lost their homes. Not hillbillies, not characters or caricatures, but people. People whose lives had been upended. People who had been hit hard by something they didn't expect.

There will likely always be smug naysayers like Bill O'Reilly and Nathaniel Weyl. And we certainly have not seen the end of deceptive politics, destructive industry, and natural disasters. But no matter what bullshit mountain people have to deal with, at least they have Dolly Parton.

Dolly Parton cares about the mountains, she cares about the culture there—and, yes, she cares about the hillbillies and the white trash too. That is why those terms sound different coming out of her mouth. You don't get to throw those terms around and wrap yourself up in them unless you care. You have got to be invested. I won't say that you have to have lived it, because everyone's experience is different. Dolly Parton *has* lived it, but that is only a little part of what matters. The most important thing is that she seems to really care. She didn't just leave it all behind. She could have. It would have been easy for Parton to strike out for Nashville and never look back. Many performers who find early stardom leave their childhoods behind. Think of Michael Jackson and Gary, Indiana, or Bob Dylan and Duluth, Minnesota. Buck Owens was eager to escape his Dust Bowl Texas youth, then he got to Bakersfield, California, and he was never associated with anyplace else. But Parton has never been able—or never wanted—to leave her mountains behind.

Pancakes, Paula Deen, and the Pigeon Forge Parkway

I've made a fortune looking cheap.

—**Dolly Parton**[1]

SEPARATING DOLLYWOOD from Pigeon Forge and Gatlinburg is impossible. Dollywood, thanks to its matriarch, has deliberate and positive depictions of mountain fantasy, but Dolly Parton's positivity doesn't always extend beyond the gates of her theme park. If Dollywood carefully dances along the edge of oversimplification, the Pigeon Forge Parkway leaps into the crevasse of stereotype without a second thought. To drive down the parkway today is to be immersed in the neon smear of transient consumer culture that rolls south to the gates of the national park. The outsized buildings and overdeveloped hotels, tourist attractions, and chain restaurants begin at the edge of the national park and flow through Gatlinburg and Pigeon Forge along Route 441, aka the parkway. In some places the parkway is eight lanes wide and surrounded by staggeringly gaudy tourist attractions—wax museums, Ferris wheels, and miniature golf courses. The signage is bright, and countless statues and novelties try to lure tourists off the highway and into their parking lots. The effect is something like the Las Vegas Strip, only without gambling, sex, or, until recently, much drinking. The parkway is a chaste Vegas.

You can see an upside-down mansion called Wonder Works that looks a bit like the White House. Wonder Works also owns attractions in other destinations, including Myrtle Beach and Orlando. Near the topsy-turvy White House is a half-scale replica of the *Titanic*, complete with a sculpted concrete iceberg. The *Titanic* of Pigeon Forge claims to be the "World's Largest Titanic Museum Attraction." Its website describes what sounds like a kind of grim funhouse: "As visitors touch a real iceberg, walk the Grand Staircase and third class hallways, reach their hands into 28-degree water, and try to stand on the sloping decks, they learn what it was like on the RMS *Titanic* by experiencing it first-hand."[2]

The Hollywood Wax Museum features a life-size King Kong climbing a faux Empire State Building. The other side of the museum building is sculpted to look like a three-story Mount Rushmore featuring Elvis, Marilyn Monroe, John Wayne, and Charlie Chaplin.

Next on the strip are giant castles, countless go-kart tracks, and a Christmas-themed hotel where the rooms have decorated trees year round—the honeymoon suite is uncomfortably named the Mr. and Mrs. Claus room. The dozens of dinner theaters have a range of themes. Country music seems to be the most popular, naturally, but one features hillbilly comedy, another the Bible, and various musical family shows would feel right at home here or in Branson, Missouri, or anywhere where "inoffensive," "old-fashioned," and "passé" might be taken as compliments.

Of course, the Dixie Stampede sells Dolly's vanilla version of the War between the States. In 2015 Parton announced she was adding another dinner attraction to her portfolio: Lumberjack Adventure. She closed the old attraction and revamped and remodeled the theater. In what could be seen as a move away from hillbilly caricature, Parton rechristened the show Dolly Parton's Smoky Mountain Adventures Dinner and Show. Tourism websites describe the new show as "some incredible new acts designed specifically for the theatre stage. With the backdrop of Dolly's music and tapestry of characters, the Owens and the Partons will do battle for the Pigeon Forge mill. . . . The story unfolds of a family that shaped the future of the Great Smoky Mountains in East Tennessee."[3]

A few throwbacks to the original waves of Pigeon Forge development remain, such as the Smoky Mountain Pancake House. At the recently shuttered Hill-Billy Village, visitors could buy mammy figurines and rebel flag doormats, as recently as 2016, before visiting a supposedly genuine moonshine still at the back of the attraction. That still, which didn't function—and kind of looked like it never did—became eclipsed by functioning stills farther down the parkway.

In 2010, in an effort to increase the tax base, lawmakers legalized distilling in Sevier County. This created a significant new market in a county that had traditionally been largely dry. In the years since legalization Pigeon Forge and Gatlinburg have seen an average of four moonshine distilleries open each year, mostly on US 441. Some of the larger legal moonshiners have even opened second locations and are beginning to sell their products in other counties and even other states.

Ole Smoky Distillery was the first of these operations. It now has two large locations, one in Gatlinburg and one in Pigeon Forge. Ole Smoky—and all the other nouveau 'shine houses—have a strikingly deliberate rustic feel. All the products are sold in mason jars, and every one of East Tennessee's new distilleries has a label that attempts to look handmade, letterpress, or roughhewn. All but a few have flavors that are intensely sweet and often fruity. Sweet classics include apple pie, and among the other varieties are pink watermelon, neon green sour apple, and cherry. All the Gatlinburg and Pigeon Forge distilleries (eight at last count, with more likely to open) use large raw wooden showrooms with ample bars for sampling. Some even go so far as to stage their storefronts with hay bales and antique farm equipment. The idea is to tap into a feeling of heritage and authenticity to sell white corn liquor in the mountains. One distillery, Doc Collier Moonshine of Gatlinburg, tells visitors that after they taste the product, "you can see some of the equipment that William 'Doc' Collier and his family have used for generations to make their moonshine up in the mountains." Another, Sugarlands Distilling Company, whose storefront distillery was made from wood salvaged from local barns and farmhouses, offers meet-and-greets with "authentic moonshiners," who offer autographed jars of such products as Mark Rogers' American Peach or Jim Tom Hedrick's Unaged Rye. Ole Smoky, which is endorsed by the country musician Dierks Bentley, proclaims that its heritage comes from "hollers deep and hidden, from plowing dark earth and corn growing tall."[4] Unlike many of the new developments, these businesses aren't ignoring the region and they aren't exactly obfuscating its history, like the souvenir stores that sell Confederate flag merchandise. These distilleries don't feel exactly like part of a local food movement either. There is something too studied and too polished about their presentation. They are so desperate to grasp at something that resembles authenticity that everything about them feels hopelessly artificial. They are hyperreal. It feels, like so much of Gatlinburg and Pigeon Forge, that they too are selling just another fantasy.

The old venues are quickly becoming relics; national and international brands are moving onto the parkway, each with a larger sign and fancier building than the next. Each has another fantasy to pawn off on a seemingly willing public, and unlike the blue raspberry–flavored moonshine barns, these new folks don't even pretend to care about the landscape around them. In May 2014 a Hard Rock Cafe opened, and about a month later Jimmy Buffett's Margaritaville Restaurant opened in a large commercial development called The Island.[5]

Buffett was riding a wave of new development in the county. These developers, almost all outsiders, are building larger and larger brands that are increasingly disconnected from the mountain image that has been cultivated for decades. The Margaritaville Hotel and Restaurant is designed to make visitors feel as though they are on a Caribbean beach, right down to floor treatments printed to look like sand. The lobby of Buffett's Margaritaville restaurant goes so far as to use artificial palm trees and murals instead of windows. In his restaurant the mountains are not just ignored, like at the Hard Rock Cafe or the *Titanic* attraction. In Margaritaville the mountains are a visual obstacle to the restaurant's philosophy. To see the actual locale reminds visitors too much of where they actually are, and the reality of the restaurant comes crashing into their consciousness.

I think Dolly's relationship to all this is a little fuzzy. I'm not sure exactly where she fits in. She's a part of this place—it is her place, her town as much as anyone's. She didn't put a business with her name on it in a tourist trap town just to make a few bucks—she came from that town. Tourist attractions have been here at least as long as Parton has been alive. Everything about how she presents this place, this culture, and maybe herself is colored by the experience of growing up just down the road from the progenitors of places like Margaritaville. No wonder she's such a good saleswoman. Growing up here must have convinced Parton of just how valuable the ability to sell fantasy could be.

See, as much as there is joy in fantasy, it can, after a while, start to feel like a lie. As joyous a figure as Parton is on this landscape, here on the parkway she begins to feel like just another huckster with something expensive to sell. It's a depressing thought. I remind myself of Parton's connection to this region and tell myself I'm really not being fair. I feel a bit better, but I'm still depressed. I need a drink—but will it cheer me up to have a "5 O'Clock Somewhere" margarita or a moonshine piña colada?

Paula Deen's Family Kitchen restaurant is next door to Margaritaville. Deen's restaurant represents something of a comeback for this popular, yet controversial, culinary celebrity. In 2010 former employees' complaints of a pattern of racist abuse led to a heavily publicized lawsuit that was ultimately dismissed.[6] The fallout, however, was dramatic. Outrage at Deen's practices—particularly her admission in court that she used racial epithets when describing African Americans—led to her being dismissed by the Food Network and the loss of prominent sponsorships. Of equal significance was the subsequent collapse of Deen's restaurant empire, including restaurants in Georgia and many locations in casinos across the country. Paula Deen's Family Kitchen represents Deen's first new restaurant since the scandal. It is a massive venture, with more than twenty thousand square feet and a budget of nearly $20 million.[7]

I'm afraid it says something uncomfortable about what Pigeon Forge has become that Deen and her backers feel it is a safe place for a divisive figure to attempt to resurrect her restaurant career. After all, Deen's association with Savannah and the Low Country seems at odds with the traditional ethos of the mountains. It feels like the antebellum planter class is back to take the cure. Deen's version of the South is completely different from Parton's. Deen sells the "Old South"—think magnolias, colonial architecture, and cotillions. Her South seems a world away from Parton's cabins, mountains, and barn dances, and yet here it is.

~

The summer of 2015 was a strange time to be considering Deen and her return from racial discord. In June a white supremacist entered the Emanuel African Methodist Episcopal Church in Charleston, South Carolina, and killed nine African Americans who were holding a prayer meeting.[8]

The by-product of the terrorist attack in Charleston was that southern symbology, particularly the Confederate flag, was thrust into the spotlight. Suddenly it no longer was the kind of thing that could be tolerated flapping away at barbecue restaurants and souvenirs stands. After the Charleston shooting many understood that flag was not merely referencing old ideas but continuing to inspire violence.

The outcry at southern whites' continuing acceptance of the flag and Confederate monuments resulted in a remarkable moment. On July 10, 2015, the State of South Carolina removed the Confederate flag that had flown at the state capitol since 1962, when white politicians and racists like Maurice Bessinger embraced the flag as a symbol of resistance to integration.[9] Removing that flag from South Carolina's statehouse was a watershed moment, symbolically on par with the election of Barack Obama. A sign, made by a supporter of the flag's removal, read CHANGE HAS COME, echoing Obama's 2008 "Change" campaign slogan. It was a wholly and completely symbolic gesture—the people of South Carolina woke up to the same frustrations and tensions the following morning, but symbols, especially these symbols, matter.

Elsewhere other Confederate symbols, particularly at southern colleges and universities, were reassessed. But the rebel flag seems to have a knack for survival. In particular, it seems to appear when people are at leisure. The flag still waves at hunting camps, beaches, sporting events, and, yes—in Pigeon Forge and Gatlinburg.

When I went to Paula Deen's Family Kitchen, it had been open for a couple of months, but South Carolina's flag had come down the week before. I entered the crowded lobby of the restaurant, which features a re-creation of one of Deen's kitchens, along with thousands of souvenirs and kitchen items. The actual restaurant is on the second floor, and you take an escalator to get to it. Given what had transpired the week before in South Carolina, I wasn't expecting to see the person in front of me was wearing a rebel flag shirt, although it didn't surprise me. As the line grew shorter, the flag blended into the crowd, just another shirt on just another tourist. Given Deen's history, I thought about whether the flag—or Deen's very presence in Pigeon Forge—might have some greater meaning. I wondered whether the man wearing the shirt was from around here and, if so, whether his family had fought against secession? I don't think it matters. At most, the actual Civil War has a tangential relationship to the Confederate flag that has become so tied up in regionalism, politics, segregation, and white supremacy that its relationship to those movements and ideologies far outweighs any ties it may have to history or some notion of heritage.

So, what does some guy wearing that flag the week after it came down in response to racial terrorism have to do with Paula Deen's big Pigeon Forge comeback? Well, it's complicated.

Deen's three-hundred-seat restaurant and four thousand square feet of retail space are part of a huge push by Deen to create a presence in the mountains. The rollout began more than a year earlier with a series of live cooking presentations at a convention center. Next, she opened a retail store in Gatlinburg, followed a year later by her behemoth restaurant-retail installation a few miles away. The stores and restaurant marked the first major expansion of Deen's brand since her disgrace.

In a 2013 deposition Deen admitted to using racial epithets, administering a workplace rife with sexual harassment, and wanting black staffers "to play the role of slaves in a wedding party she was planning." The cultural fallout from these revelations was swift, decisive, and fierce. Deen was promptly fired from the Food Network. Smithfield Foods, the pork superproducer, also terminated its relationship with Deen. Other companies that cut ties with Deen included Target, Sears, Walgreens, and the manufacturer of a diabetes medicine. Deen's restaurants in Caesar's casinos in Mississippi, North Carolina, Indiana, Illinois, and Tennessee were all shuttered, and her association was terminated.[10]

Some observers pointed out the irony that Deen, a white southern woman, had profited by eliminating, or at least obscuring, the cultural imprint of the black cooks who had pivotal roles in the development and preparation of the southern cuisine she presented. The culinary historian Michael Twitty, writing in at the height of the scandal, noted that Deen was part of a long pattern of "culinary injustice where some Southerners take credit for things that enslaved Africans and their descendants played key roles in innovating."[11]

It is telling, perhaps, that Deen felt that the Smokies would be a safe place to stage a comeback. Perhaps Deen and her advisers felt that in catering to a largely white, overwhelmingly southern, clientele she would find a more sympathetic audience. Perhaps they hoped that the strong religious influence of the region would create an environment prone to forgiveness. It is also possible that Deen's remaining audience simply doesn't feel that she did anything wrong and overlaps with the large and lucrative crowds that patronize Sevier County.

〜

At the Pancake Pantry in Gatlinburg, Tennessee, you can feel like a VIP just by being half of a couple. The restaurant, like every restaurant in the area, is so used to serving large family groups that a couple can get seated at a puny table for two almost instantly, no matter how long the line. My wife and I got a table with a view of the kitchen, which was a lucky thing. It is remarkable to watch hundreds, if not thousands, of pancakes roll out. Overlooking the kitchen is, simply put, one of the most incredible sights in American food service: the Pancake Pantry's butter station. Behind a small counter that somewhat resembles a pulpit, a man manages stainless-steel mixing bowls filled with extraordinary amounts of whipped butter. As the wait staff picks up meals, they stop at the butter pulpit for a more-than-generous dollop before delivering the plates.

The Pancake Pantry's butter pulpit may have some serious competition in the butter tourism industry of the Smokies. Paula Deen didn't plant her flag in Pigeon Forge just to resurrect her crumbled empire. She also plopped a big old gift shop in downtown Gatlinburg just down the road from the Pancake Pantry. As at the restaurant in Pigeon Forge, her ardent fans in the gift shop excitedly buy Christmas ornaments shaped like butter sticks, plates and shirts emblazoned with "Butter Y'all," and butter-flavored lip gloss. I guess if something is worth doing around here, it is worth overdoing.

Paula Deen may have made some inroads, and of course this is Dolly Parton's town we're talking about, but neither can claim the signature food of Sevier County. At least so far as tourists are concerned, the essential delicacy of East Tennessee is the pancake. Sure, pancakes are everywhere in every state and probably in every country of the world, so what claim do Pigeon Forge and Gatlinburg have to these syrup sponges? Well, like so much in a tourist-centered economy, the claim doesn't come from the towns but from the tourists happily gulping down pancake after pancake.

Tourism came to Gatlinburg first, thanks to the national park and the construction in the 1950s of Highway 71, a route from North Carolina to what was then Coal Creek, Tennessee (it coincides with US 441 for most of its length in Tennessee).[12] Highway-building progressives felt that paving new roads through the mountains would be a key to prosperity for the region. Arguably, in the twentieth century the federal government was the most important player in the development of mountain tourism. In addition to the highways and the national park, the two factors most important to bringing people into the Smokies, the federal government provided utilities by establishing the Tennessee Valley Authority. Formation of the park and the TVA were part of the Roosevelt administration's New Deal in the 1930s.[13] The next major government-assisted boon to Sevier County's tourism industry came as a result of President Johnson's War on Poverty in the 1960s, which led to the creation of the Appalachian Regional Commission (ARC). ARC provided municipal grants to construct and update utilities and infrastructure in Gatlinburg and in Pigeon Forge.[14] The commission also provided funding for hospitality training at trade schools across the border in North Carolina.

Today, the commission remains actively involved in promoting tourism. ARC argues that "tourism development can be an important part of a community's strategy for building a sustainable economic future. Many

Appalachian communities have developed successful tourism strategies based on the Region's cultural heritage, history, and natural beauty." Dollywood is among the locations listed in ARC's guide to geotourism, defined by the National Geographic Society as "tourism that sustains or enhances the geographical character of a place—its environment, culture, aesthetics, and heritage—and the well-being of its residents."[15]

Paralleling the federal efforts was a more universal shift in the way that Americans approached their leisure time. The popularity of automobile travel made possible by better roads and the increased availability of cars across economic classes made a visit to the mountains a possibility for hundreds of thousands, if not millions, more Americans than could have visited before the age of the auto. Additionally, the rise of the middle class after World War II created a whole new group that had leisure time and disposable income to spend in destinations like Pigeon Forge and Gatlinburg.[16]

The infrastructure for the postwar tourism boom had been determined during the 1920s when local business leaders concerned about the collapse of the logging industry settled on tourism as a new form of economic stimulus. Developers, including Goldrush Junction's Art Modell, saw an opportunity in the Smoky Mountains.

Given the influence of outsiders in the Smoky Mountains after the war, perhaps it was fitting that a couple from Indiana opened what is probably the single most important restaurant in the region's history. Their place, the Pancake Pantry, is as responsible as any for the local popularity of pancakes. So far as I can tell, it is the ultimate Smoky Mountain pancake house. In 1960 June and Jim Gerding, who had vacationed in Gatlinburg in previous years, got a tip that a restaurant property was for sale along US 441 in downtown Gatlinburg. Jim Gerding had been a business major at Indiana University and had no real restaurant experience. But he thought he had a pretty good idea. "I saw a pancake house in San Francisco airport and at that time they were not very common," Gerding told the *Mountain Press*.[17]

The Gerdings hired a chef from Cincinnati and decided they would serve only breakfast. A stack of pancakes cost 55 cents, coffee a dime, and—as a special treat—blueberry waffles commanded 95 cents. The first day the Gerdings' new venture took in $41.88. It was enough, just enough, for them to stay open another day. Days turned into weeks and weeks turned into fifty-five years. The Pancake Pantry remains open and successful. You can spot the restaurant not so much by its signage but by the lines that stretch down the sidewalk of Gatlinburg's main drag. The wait on a summer weekend morning can be more than an hour, which is remarkable, considering the restaurant seats almost two hundred.[18]

The menu at the Pancake Pantry greets the diner with twenty-four cartoon cast-iron skillets, each with a different item written inside. The offerings range from the pretty standard—wild blueberry pancakes or buttermilk pancakes—to the more adventurous: Apricot-Lemon Delight and the wonderfully named Banana Pineapple Triumph. The Pancake Pantry also serves omelets and even cereal, but they are relegated to the fine print at the side of the menu and face stiff competition, such as the sweet potato pancakes, a crowd favorite.

But a successful restaurant is only a piece of the entrepreneurial Hoosiers' legacy. When the Gerdings opened the Pancake Pantry, Sevier County had no other pancake restaurants. In fact, the Gerdings believe they opened the first pancake restaurant in the entire state of Tennessee. In 2015 a Google search found seven restaurants with *pancake* in their name in Gatlinburg alone and another eight in Pigeon Forge. If you Google "Pancake capital of the world," Gatlinburg features in three of the top five results. (Lubbock, Texas, and Hawai'i also feature prominently.)

With the exception of the International House of Pancakes on the Pigeon Forge Parkway, most of the pancake houses are still locally owned. They form a scant bulwark against the hundreds of chain establishments that have surrounded them in recent decades. The parkway section of US 441, which serves as the main street for tourists through both Pigeon Forge and Gatlinburg, has become a preposterous neon ode to staggering amounts of development.

Leon Downey, the director of Pigeon Forge's department of tourism, has also noticed the change. "You have outside businesses who want to take advantage of that traffic, that's why you have Jimmy Buffet and Paula Deen interested," he said, adding that the industry is fluid, and fast paced—contrary to any conception of a quiet mountain town. "It is never static—in the twenty-six years that I've been here it's been constant development and redevelopment."[19]

While the flux and sheen of the parkway stand in clear contrast to the national park, they also, perhaps surprisingly, stand in contrast to Dollywood. "To me, we're not the Parkway . . . it's not good versus bad, but people who don't have an affinity for that think we are more of that—that becomes a challenge," said Tim Berry, vice president of Dollywood.[20] He sees Dollywood as a mediator between the two poles of the national park and the parkway: "A lot of people come to the Smoky Mountains and don't have the ability to hike very far or don't have the stamina to do a full-blown trail. What we provide is that sense of adventure in a controlled environment." Berry explained that Dollywood gives people who are not interested in nature the *sense* of being in the national park. This allows people to convince themselves that they have experienced something that they have not. A visitor to Dollywood might get an idea of what it's like to raft in a mountain stream by riding the River Rush at the water park Splash Country. Instead of having to hike through Cades Cove to see the Baptist church, tourists can experience a reasonable facsimile on the grounds of the theme park. Perhaps—like tourists so often do—they would prefer the facsimile to the real thing. It's hard to believe that people actually think that by riding a theme-park attraction they are having a "mountain experience," but some undoubtedly enjoy being told that, having seen the theme park, they can skip the mountain hike.

The tourist towns of Sevier County have sold fantasy for quite some time. Fantasy is a shortcut to marketing success. It can comfort and it can reaffirm. The idealized mountain South sold in Pigeon Forge and Gatlinburg doesn't attempt to challenge stereotypes. Most vendors there seem to assume that offering the simplest narrative is the surest way to the hearts and wallets of their patrons.

The familiar can provide great comfort; the Pancake Pantry proves this every day that it has a line out the door. But the fear of alienating customers by avoiding complex narratives and challenges to ingrained assumptions has allowed Pigeon Forge to become an increasingly reactionary vacation destination. Will some of the recent trends, represented by Paula Deen and the moonshine distilleries, continue, or will a new appetite develop for something more inclusive and more grounded in the singular location that the mountains represent?

Okra, Chicken Livers, and a Break for Dinner

Anything I've got would fit at Cracker Barrel! 'cause they're country
and I'm country. I'm a good cook and they're a good cook
and we cook the same kind of food!

—Dolly Parton[1]

LIKE MOST Cracker Barrels, the parking lot of the one in Pigeon Forge was crowded. A sign read, A NEIGHBORLY REMINDER: LOCK YOUR CAR AND REMOVE YOUR VALUABLES.

It was like every Cracker Barrel I've ever set foot in. Perhaps the most distinguishing characteristic of the Cracker Barrel on the Pigeon Forge Parkway is that it could be anywhere. Every other chain along that road seems to be trying to live up to the outsized attractions.

Every restaurant seems to be a bigger, bolder, more bodacious version of the chain it represents. Not Cracker Barrel. As we walked into the Old Country Store, we could've been walking into the location in Merrillville, Indiana, or Greensboro, North Carolina, or Parkersburg, West Virginia.

We walked past the plastic bric-a-brac and shelves of retro candy and sweets that lead to the dining room. A hostess greeted us with a smile. A bearded man wearing overalls and a canvas chore coat added logs to a roaring fire. The wood smoke mingled with the scent of biscuits. We were seated next to a table where a woman was opening a gift from a friend; at another table an elderly man was making friendly small talk with the folks at the table next to his. A half-dozen women wearing pink-and-black smocks arrived soon after we did. As they laughed and carried on for a brief moment, the smell of perms and perfume overwhelmed the aroma of food and fire—clearly, they were hairdressers taking a lunch break. A high school class photo from the early 1900s and an old hunting advertisement hung on the wall next to our table. Next to it was an old ad for RC Cola in glass bottles, like the ones sold by the cash registers at the front of the restaurant.

People seemed at home there. We felt at home too. More than six hundred fires roar in stone fireplaces at Cracker Barrels across the country. Six hundred hosts stand in the same spot next to six hundred displays of old-fashioned candy. Across America, a few yards from every major interstate from Maine to Florida and from North Carolina to Arizona, the power of Cracker Barrel lies in that consistency—the ability to create a comforting, predictable experience with exactly the same branded narrative.

It's not so different from the feeling I get at Dollywood. They evoke the same sense of nostalgia—a feeling of comfort for something I've never experienced. It's a weird feeling, one that shouldn't make sense—but I kind of like it. The difference, of course, is that Cracker Barrel isn't connected to a place. The aesthetic and the food are deeply rooted in Tennessee, but that would matter only if Cracker Barrel had restaurants in only its home state. Dollywood brings people to Appalachia and shows them what it thinks they ought to see. Cracker Barrel brings a vague notion of Tennessee to people all over the country.

Looking around that dining room, I was struck by how Cracker Barrel had ceased to be a replica of a country store and gathering place and had become the real thing. People make meaning out of this place. The story of Cracker Barrel is that of a manufactured, branded narrative that customers consume and adopt as their own. It is also the story of a marketed, imagined South of the past as well as in the present. The spread of Cracker Barrel mirrors the southernization of the United States, a trend marked by the spread of rural conservatism, religious values, nationalism, and also a longing for the imagined history of a misremembered region.[2] Cracker Barrel also shows us the power of redefinition. The customers who enjoy this experience increasingly are less nostalgic for memories of long-gone country stores and home-cooked meals than for their own memories of past meals enjoyed at Cracker Barrel, usually en route to someplace. For many the imitation has become the genuine.

Cracker Barrel—like Dollywood—wouldn't exist without the Interstate Highway System. In her book *Dixie Highway,* Tammy Ingram argues that building the interstates was "a crucial lynchpin in the transition to the modern South, a transition that shaped its political institutions as well as its infrastructure."[3] Ingram also points out that the interstates led to profound cultural changes. The Dixie Highway in her book's title was a kind progenitor of the postwar system developed in the 1950s. The Dixie Highway—actually a network of several highways—brought thousands of tourists from Lake Michigan to Miami with hundreds of stops (including the Great Smoky Mountains) along the way. This not only opened lines of communication between southerners and their neighbors in the Midwest but created a dialog about the usefulness of roads.

The most famous, and certainly most successful, advocate for the development of a modern highway system was Dwight Eisenhower. He framed the issue as a defense initiative, but it also grew out of a desire to modernize the country. Eisenhower had participated in the Motor Transport Corps of 1919, a massive military convoy designed to both test and exhibit the motor vehicle on the three thousand miles from Washington, DC, to San Francisco. The journey took about two months. Eisenhower's proposal would cut that travel time down to less than a week—helpful in the event of an invasion, sure, but more in helpful in terms of creating a modern, mobile America.

In the 1960s a Consolidated Oil employee named Dan Evins traveled the interstates, which were still fairly new at the time, as an oil jobber. Oil jobbers marketed fuel from the big refineries to gas stations and industrial operators, and Evins was feeling nostalgic for what he thought of as the classic southern country store.

Evins came from a well-connected southern family of aspiring middle-class whites. His uncle was Joe L. Evins, a Tennessean who served in the US House of Representatives for thirty years. He had taken Al Gore Sr.'s seat in the House when Gore was elected to the Senate. Evins was mostly an old-fashioned Tennessee Democrat, though he made waves in 1956 when he became one of the few southern Democrats to break with the Dixiecrats because of his opposition to the "Southern Manifesto" against racial integration (specifically the 1954 Supreme Court decision in *Brown v. Board of Education*). Evins later was a patron of the Appalachian Center for Craft at Tennessee Technical University.

After attending Auburn University and serving in the Korean War, Dan Evins worked as a congressional aide for his uncle before joining the family oil business. According to company lore, Dan quickly grew tired of life on the road—particularly the food: "Fast food might be a good business idea, Dan thought, but it sure wasn't such a hot eating idea. Truth is, Dan always saw mealtime as special—a time to catch up with your family, your friends, and your thoughts. Meals weren't meant to be swallowed down in three bites with a squirt of ketchup."[4]

Evins thought that the antidote would be to bring back something he remembered from his childhood but that was fast disappearing from the landscape: the country store. The folksy narrative on Cracker Barrel's website explains, "Dan figured maybe folks traveling on the big new highways might appreciate a clean, comfortable, relaxed place to stop in for a good meal and some shopping that would offer up unique gifts and self-indulgences, many reminiscent of America's country heritage."[5] With the newly built Interstate 40 running right through his hometown, Evins tested his theory at one of his family's gas stations. In 1969 he rebuilt the station with expanded retail space and a full-service restaurant. He mimicked the architectural vernacular of a country store with a large sign in a western-style font, board-and-batten paneling, and a long front porch filled with rocking chairs. A sign on the storefront advertised GOOD COUNTRY COOKIN. The new venture was quickly a success. Located in Evins's hometown of Lebanon, at the intersection of I-40 and Highway 109, the store provided hot meals, gasoline, and a place to take a break. Evins wanted the original menu to be homespun and guileless—in the dialect of rural white flatlanders and mountain hillbillies—and it was almost overwhelmingly so, riddled with intentional misspellings and backward letters: "If'n you need anything that ain't on here hollar at tha cook." One side of the menu featured "Brakfast" with "Aigs," "biscits," ham, and sawmill gravy on one side. The other side offered "Sanwiches," burgers, and Cracker Barrel's specialties: country ham and "buiscuits," county line cheese and crackers, "'lonies" (bologna to you Yankees) and crackers, a bowl of beans with ham hock and cornbread, and greens and "hawg jowl." On the back of the menu was a primer for word-of-mouth advertising, "Take this here menu with ya 'n if'n ya'll liked these vittles tell yore nabors 'n hope us out. If'n you didn't—well these here menus have graced better outhouses 'n yourn."

Evins played to his audience like a vaudevillian and it worked. Legend has it that Cracker Barrel made a profit after its first month. Evins opened a second restaurant in Manchester, Tennessee, within a year.[6] Soon after that he opened additional stores in Harriman, Tennessee, and Franklin, Kentucky. The first four restaurants opened along interstates, two on I-40, one on I-65, and the fourth on I-24. Even today nearly all six hundred Cracker Barrel restaurants are located along interstates.

In choosing these locales Evins was counterbalancing the modernity of Eisenhower's interstates with nostalgia. Cracker Barrels offset the gleaming chrome modernity of America's first fast-food restaurants—such as McDonald's in California and Krispy Kreme in North Carolina—with the homespun décor of wood and country antiques. He put oil lamps on every table and with them Cracker Barrel's famous pegboard solitaire game, Jump All But One. The text on the games still recalls Evins's original menu, telling diners: "Jump each tee and remove it. Leave only one—you're genius. Leave two and you're purty smart. Leave three and you're just plain dumb. Leave four or mor'n you're just plain 'eg-no-ra-moose.'" Playing a board game adds to the "come set a spell" atmosphere so expertly crafted by Cracker Barrel.

Today, Larry Singleton, the chain's décor manager, creates much of Cracker Barrel's evocative atmosphere. The Cracker Barrel Old Country Store Décor Warehouse is an enormous repository of antiques, artifacts, and Americana at Cracker Barrel headquarters in Lebanon, Tennessee. Company literature stresses that each Cracker Barrel store is decorated with "real American artifacts, memorabilia, and signage."[7] This authenticity is an essential aspect of Cracker Barrel's narrative. The place is, after all, a construct. It is crucial that customers perceive the décor as real because this is a brand that markets authenticity. Michael Beverland, who teaches marketing at RMIT University in Melbourne, argues in his book *Building Brand Authenticity* that when many consumers feel rootless because of globalization, branding can "keep personally relevant identity narratives alive."[8]

In other words, in the twenty-first century many of our identities have become so generic that the most efficient way to create an identity is to buy stuff.

Imagine, if you will, a youngish person who was born in northern Mississippi. This fictional person graduated from high school and went to college out of state, say, to Northwestern University in Evanston, Illinois. Then she got a job in Philadelphia and made her adult life in the suburbs of that city. Those three distinct places all blur together. Maybe in Philadelphia she buys local brands or she goes the opposite way, consuming products associated with Chicago. Maybe she gets homesick for the South from time to time and goes to King of Prussia to have a meal at Cracker Barrel—not a taste of home so much as a brand from home.

This is exactly why Cracker Barrel means so much to the people who care about the region. The South *feels* authentic there—even outside the South. To enter a Cracker Barrel is to enter a timeless and largely amorphous space. It is vaguely rural and distinctly backward looking. Cracker Barrel describes its look as Americana. In *It Still Moves,* an exploration of the musical genre also known as Americana, Amanda Petrusich describes a visit to a Cracker Barrel in Washington, DC: "*Americana,* employed as a marketing term, is more about employing fuzzy formless warmth. . . . We are buying into the artifacts of activities and emotions most of us have never experienced firsthand. These objects, and not memories or facts, are the greatest players in the classic Americana myth."[9]

This mythos is the power of Cracker Barrel. Entering *any* store takes us to a comfortable imaginary place. Cracker Barrels are like tiny theme parks dotting America's interstates: every exit brings the opportunity not to travel back in time but to travel to what was once a whole new kind of space. It didn't feel new because all its touchstones are familiar. For the generations born immediately before and after World War II, Cracker Barrel echoed country stores, Grandma's house, country cafes, and other homespun touchstones. Of course, if you're younger than that, Cracker Barrel evokes nostalgia by reminding us of . . . Cracker Barrel.

This is what Cracker Barrel and Dollywood have in common. They have been around long enough, and done what they do well enough, that the cultural signifiers they reference have nearly faded out of sight. The imitated thing has become the only thing for an entire generation or two. I never went to country stores with my grandparents—certainly not one that sold old-fashioned candy and had oil lamps. I don't think there was much of a market for oil lamps in the eighties. I did go to Cracker Barrel with them, a lot. They've passed now, but I can still recite my grandfather's order from memory: fried chicken livers or catfish with hash brown casserole. He'd ask if they could put the casserole on the griddle and brown it on both sides—a request that embarrassed me at the time, although I'm not sure why. For dessert he'd have a frozen mug sundae with almonds instead of peanuts. I had mine without nuts. Those memories—that rush of nostalgia is real to me. That nostalgia counts, just as it does when it evokes memories of actual country stores.

～

By the end of the 1970s Cracker Barrel had discontinued its gasoline sales, initially because of the oil crisis. By 1980 the company was focused solely on family dining and gift sales. In 1981 the company went public, and Evins remained as chief executive, a role he held until 2001.

In the late 1990s Cracker Barrel determined it would open fifty stores a year. Today the company operates in forty-two states and employs more than sixty-seven thousand people.[10]

In one of its ventures Cracker Barrel has connected to Nashville's lucrative music scene, releasing exclusive recordings by Brad Paisley, Vince Gill, Smokey Robinson, the Gaither family, and the hero of this story, Dolly Parton. Cracker Barrel has become a player in the music scene, particularly in country and Christian music. A Nashville agent described the connection as one of shared purpose: "They know exactly who their customer is. Cracker Barrel sells exactly the same thing that country music does, which is familiarity and comfort."[11] The deals have been largely successful, a remarkable feat in a lagging CD market. Here it probably helps that Cracker Barrel is a road trip stop. As conversation lags and the miles pile up, a CD can become an increasingly attractive impulse buy. And the popularity of CDs may reflect a technology gap between shoppers at the Old Country Store and those who patronize other retailers. Parton's Cracker Barrel release was certified gold with all copies sold exclusively through the Old Country Stores.

It seems immediately apparent to me that Cracker Barrel is a southern icon, and certainly the company owes a great deal of its substance to the South. After all, it was classic middle Tennessee country stores that inspired Dan Evins. Cracker Barrel's menu, along with that of Kentucky Fried Chicken, contains some of the most iconic mass-market southern food available. However, in its marketing and promotion materials, Cracker Barrel is profoundly regionally neutral. The company never refers to its cuisine as southern, nor does it place its stores or products in a regional context. Instead the food is described as home cooking or country, and the products are similarly described as home-style, nostalgic, or wholesome. The neutrality is a by-product of the chain's national reach. Cracker Barrel is careful not to alienate its northern and western clientele by clinging too directly to its southern roots.

On the company website Cracker Barrel argues that, in fact, the company's roots are broader than the South and—somewhat counter-intuitively—that Cracker Barrel is inspired by everywhere: "What Dan had in mind was the kind of place he'd been to hundreds of times as a boy. It was a place called the country store, something every small community once had. Out west, they called them trading posts; up north, they were general stores. Where Dan grew up, in Middle Tennessee, they were old country stores."

In practice, Cracker Barrel is widely recognized for what it is—a studied reproduction of southern iconography. In public discourse about the restaurant, stereotypes, prejudices, and politics often seem to hinge on Cracker Barrel's southernness. Compounding the problem was a rash of public relations disasters involving accusations of discrimination during the period when the company was growing fastest.

In 1991, a cook at the Douglasville, Georgia, Cracker Barrel was fired for "showing inappropriate behavior." In fact, that behavior was being a lesbian. The cook, Cheryl Summerville, was fired because of a new company policy dictating that Cracker Barrel's employees should "demonstrate normal heterosexual values." As a result sixteen workers were fired from the chain.[12]

Summerville initially intended to sue for wrongful termination but learned that in Georgia at the time it was legal for employers to discriminate based on sexual orientation. Summerville started a boycott. Although it is difficult to say whether the boycott affected Cracker Barrel's bottom line, it certainly gained attention. She made nationally televised appearances, including on CNN's *Larry King Live*. For some people, particularly those living outside the South and the Midwest, their first exposure to Cracker Barrel was through this coverage. Within a year Cracker Barrel had dropped the discriminatory policy, and Evins publicly admitted it was a mistake.[13]

In 2004, under pressure from the US Department of Justice, Cracker Barrel adopted a stronger antidiscrimination policy in order to avoid litigation in a racial discrimination case. Two years later a legal threat from Al Sharpton's National Action Network made national news.[14]

Today every Cracker Barrel location has a large wooden sign in its entryway:

> In the spirit of pleasing people, we invite everyone regardless of race, color, disability or national origin to enjoy our restaurant and old country store. Since 1969 we have tried our best to provide food and service in ways that uphold our traditions of

genuine quality. If you feel we have not delivered on this prom-
ise, please let us know. 1-800-333-9566 or crackerbarrel.com.

This sign is a powerful mea culpa from the company, and it has an
ironic tie to southern material culture. The South, after all, has an especially sordid history of racist signage outside restaurants. Cracker
Barrel is famous for its collection of artifacts and ephemera; the chain's
antidiscrimination signs are powerful additions to that collection that
speak of racism's stranglehold on the nation.

Cracker Barrel's history of discrimination is especially powerful
because of its cultivation of a particular imaginary experience. Though
the chain distances itself from a southern identity in its promotional
language, it is impossible to ignore the essential southernisms that are
present in every Cracker Barrel. The country store is itself a southern
icon. The menu has changed a great deal since Evins's original store:
it now features a section called Wholesome Fixin's for diners looking
for option that are low calorie, vegetarian, or safe for diabetics. Despite
these updates the menu has not become a homogenized version of
highway fare; it retains unmistakably regional dishes that would have
fit right in with the original offerings of turnip greens, fried okra, country ham, and hickory-smoked barbecue.

Many Americans certainly view Cracker Barrel's problems as a re-
flection of its southern origins. As with Paula Deen, this line of thinking veers dangerously into the problem of met expectations. If the cultural expectation is that to be truly southern something has to be racist
or reactionary, some facets of southern culture will sink to meet that
expectation. If all southerners have to prove they are really and truly
southern by making an exclusionary statement, then not only can the
southern identity become a hurtful one (a huge problem in its own
right) but the South itself ceases to have any ability to surprise, reinvent, or challenge, all of which are essential elements of being a real
place—not just a brand.

It is difficult to calculate whether Cracker Barrel has been hurt by
its link to the South or if, in fact, the opposite is true. Cracker Barrel's southern identity hurts and helps the company in different ways.
Confirming a stereotype can often be confused with authenticity. If we

collectively believe that southerners are supposed to be reactionary or racist or exclusionary in some way, then we search for that. The problem then is that people have to fit a stereotype to be perceived as authentically southern. Is Morris Dees, for example, not really a southern man because he's a progressive? Because he's an activist? This kind of coding sets a dangerous precedent.

Cultural icons rooted in the South are spun by the pervasive complexities of the region. Those complexities are less readily apparent in places where there is less inclination toward the southern fascination with self-examination. Put more simply, why would visitors to Michigan (home to sixteen stores) care about understanding the complexities of southern politics? The answer is that they don't. What they care about is the cultural coding that equates southernness with authenticity. Dolly Parton could have grown up poor almost anywhere, but her biography might not have been as much a part of her identity if she had grown up in, say, New York State. Rare is the musician who brags about his or her midwestern roots. If a singer is from the South, that's usually the first line in their bio.

As Cracker Barrel has gained more notoriety, it has become an uncomfortable symbol of conservative white values and politics. In 2011 the *Washington Post* published an op-ed piece under the headline "Will the 2012 Election Be a Contest of Whole Foods vs. Cracker Barrel Shoppers?" The journalist David Wasserman argued that the popularity of the chains (incidentally, both are southern—Whole Foods is based in Austin) was indicative of the deepening chasm between America's blue and red states. Whole Foods represents urban, educated, European car–owning liberals, Wasserman claimed. A Cracker Barrel patron is an uneducated, rural, pickup truck–owning conservative. That gap, he contended, is reflected in our elections: "In 2008, candidate Barack Obama carried 81 percent of counties with a Whole Foods and just 36 percent of counties with a Cracker Barrel—a record 45-point gap." And Wasserman was writing three and a half years before Donald Trump began his quest to be the Republican candidate for president. Wasserman quoted Julie Davis, a Cracker Barrel representative who downplayed any link between the stores and political affiliation: "Politics don't play any role in our site selection process."[15]

But like its southern roots, the chain cannot escape politics. In advance of the January 2014 issue of *GQ*, a profile of the reality television star and hunting call inventor Phil Robertson (*Duck Dynasty*) hit the news cycle. In the profile Robertson shares his provocative brand of Christianity: "Start with homosexual behavior and just morph out from there. Bestiality, sleeping around with this woman and that woman and that woman and those men." Then he paraphrased Corinthians: "Don't be deceived. Neither the adulterers, the idolaters, the male prostitutes, the homosexual offenders, the greedy, the drunkards, the slanderers, the swindlers—they won't inherit the kingdom of God. Don't deceive yourself. It's not right."[16]

Public condemnation of these remarks was swift and decisive. A&E, the network that broadcasts Robertson's show, *Duck Dynasty*, announced his suspension. Cracker Barrel quickly followed suit, announcing via Facebook on December 20, 2013: "Cracker Barrel's mission is Pleasing People. We operate within the ideals of fairness, mutual respect and equal treatment of all people. These ideals are the core of our corporate culture." While Cracker Barrel kept some of Robertson's products on its shelves, the company's statement added, "We removed selected products which we were concerned might offend some of our guests while we evaluate the situation."

Reaction to this decision was instant and overwhelmingly negative, highlighting the complexity of selling southern nostalgia in the twenty-first century. "After you are done removing the selected products, go ahead and remove a bunch of tables and chairs . . . you won't be needing them any more," responded one commenter. Many threatened to take their business to Chik-Fil-A, the Georgia-based fast-food chain whose founder had expressed views similar to Robertson's months before. Two days after posting its initial message, Cracker Barrel issued an open letter to its customers:

> Dear Cracker Barrel Customer:
>
> When we made the decision to remove and evaluate certain *Duck Dynasty* items, we offended many of our loyal customers. Our intent was to avoid offending, but that's just what we've done.

You told us we made a mistake. And, you weren't shy about it. You wrote, you called and you took to social media to express your thoughts and feelings. You flat out told us we were wrong.

We listened.

Today, we are putting all our *Duck Dynasty* products back in our stores.

And, we apologize for offending you.

We respect all individuals right to express their beliefs. We certainly did not mean to have anyone think different.

We sincerely hope you will continue to be part of our Cracker Barrel family.

Employees were given similar scripts for dealing with irate customers at the restaurants. They were told to say, "I'm sorry you are disappointed in us."[17]

It was clearly a panicked move. Cracker Barrel corporate executives believed their customer base had changed. By attempting to move past its history of discrimination, Cracker Barrel had alienated a vocal group that clearly felt that Cracker Barrel was their place, a place free from challenge to their beliefs, a place where they could be affirmed. They clearly didn't believe the company line in the *Washington Post* op-ed. Suddenly Cracker Barrel was at the heart of the American culture wars.

In entering the cultural fight and establishing a place, deserved or not, as an icon in the recurring argument, Cracker Barrel found itself in a place that Dolly Parton never seems to find herself. Parton is generally quite adept at steering clear of the controversies that pop up on cable news networks. At a time when even saying, "Happy holidays" can create a public furor, hers is an incredible achievement. What's even more remarkable is Parton's ability to defuse controversy in the rare instances that it does make an appearance.

The first time I visited Dollywood, a woman wearing a T-shirt in support of gay marriage was asked to turn the shirt inside out before entering the water park. After she protested, the story gained national attention. Parton stepped in to apologize: "I am truly sorry for the hurt or embarrassment regarding the gay and lesbian T-shirt incident at Dollywood's Splash Country recently. Everyone knows of my personal support of the gay and lesbian community. Dollywood is a family park and all families are welcome."[18] Many commentators pointed out that guests had never been turned away for wearing T-shirts displaying the Confederate flag.

Kim Severson observes this tension in her piece about Dollywood in the *New York Times*: "That Dolly Parton, 68, is also a gay icon would probably be news to many of the guests in cargo shorts and tennis shoes who wait patiently in line each day until 'The Star Spangled Banner' is sung and the park opens. But for the rest of us, it is not." It is hard to imagine that Parton's very public relationship with the gay community has gone unnoticed by her more conservative Christian fans. As Severson points out, gays and lesbians account for some of the park's business, as well as a significant percentage of Parton's overall fan base. This is certainly not a secret in East Tennessee. Dollywood's director of public relations told me a few weeks before Severson's story was published that Parton had written an as-yet unreleased song that is friendly toward her gay fans. As Severson noted, that Parton's right-leaning fans were unaware of her relationship with the gay community speaks to her fans' sense of ownership.[19] Somehow, Parton sings hymns, sponsors evangelical gospel festivals, and supports gay rights without alienating either fan base.

Officially, Dollywood doesn't seek to exclude groups of people— not intentionally—but it does offer an experience that speaks more profoundly to some and makes some groups feel far safer than others. Attempting to create an environment free from controversy and free from offense is a fraught proposition, one that reinforces the status quo. Reducing any culture into a saleable commodity is a complex exchange. Selling the South as a popular brand is particularly complicated. The historian Charles Wilson Reagan explains: "In the South, pop culture is negotiated between tradition and modernity. It often draws from folklore, from folk symbols and rituals. But it is not so much concerned with authenticity as it is with reproducing these symbols for broad audiences."[20]

In cherry-picking pieces of southern culture to create something comfortable and marketable, Cracker Barrel succeeds in creating something new. Cracker Barrel makes real and accessible the fantasy of the

South that lives in so many southerners (and people from everywhere else too).

Jia Tolentino exquisitely articulates this connection in her "Letter of Recommendation" in the *New York Times*:

> The nostalgia sold by Cracker Barrel alongside every plate and trinket requires no previous emotional stake in the South as an institution. In my case, Cracker Barrel may have actually induced that investment in reverse. I grew up in a non-white family in white corporate Texas. And for most of my childhood, Southern fetish objects left me disturbed. I did not like going to sleepovers at houses with Confederate flags on the wall or learning to drink with boys who owned guns. The aggression in southern culture is heightened by the fact that it often passes as gentility. But Cracker Barrel makes the South seem, just briefly, like the front-porch paradise it believes itself to be.[21]

It is important that sites that serve nostalgia, like Cracker Barrel and Dollywood, speak equally to people both in and outside the regions they represent. Cracker Barrel doesn't just sell a fake version of a region. It shows us a version of the South that clings to every fantasy and tradition, both real and imagined, while steadfastly moving forward. As the signs posted at the entryway of every location firmly remind the diners, Cracker Barrel is a southern fantasy that everyone can participate in. Dollywood has no such signs at its entrance, at least not yet—but it's not hard to imagine them. Parton's public rhetoric is so inclusive that she serves as a kind of national spokesperson for the kind of progress rooted in the tradition branding that you see at Cracker Barrel.

Parton seems to be maintaining the progress part of the equation with a greater degree of grace than does Cracker Barrel—but the restaurant chain does seem to be trying. No small part of Cracker Barrel's evolution is a substantial partnership with Parton herself. You can't go into a Cracker Barrel these days without seeing Dolly everywhere. Her merchandise is well stocked in the Old Country Stores, and her music has become one of the soundtracks in the dining rooms. Parton is a fixture on the chain's social media feed too. In 2016 Parton performed her hit "Jolene" with the a capella group Pentatonix. The video of the performance, which went viral, had them performing the song in front of a faux Cracker Barrel restaurant porch. Imagine that: a replica Cracker Barrel, which itself is a replica of a country store. Perhaps in partnering with Parton Cracker Barrel has found a southern icon with far fewer thorns than the Deens and *Duck Dynasty* crews of the world.

If you can't accept Cracker Barrel's new improved image, I can't say I blame you. If you choose to decide that corporate apologies and platitudes aren't enough to make up for a history of pretty horrendous mistakes, I understand. If you feel that the word "mistake" is too tepid to describe the chain's failings, I understand that too.

I just ask that you hear me out on one thing: walking away from something doesn't always change it.

Cracker Barrel is a brand, but it is also an institution, and institutional change very often comes from within. Boycotts are most effective when loyal customers threaten to walk away from something important in their lives. Universities are more likely to listen to alumni than to outsiders. In other words, if you don't care about a thing to begin with, why should that thing care if you don't like something it does?

So my suggestion (and this doesn't just apply to Cracker Barrel, by the way) is to get in there and make yourself at home, make the place your safe space, and order a hash brown casserole like you belong—because you do.

I was in a Cracker Barrel not long ago around Christmas. The Duck Dynasty stuff was on the clearance rack and the country store had prominently displayed a collection of black Santa figurines. I'm not sure exactly what that means, but it's probably something, right?

Biography, Persona, and Reality

I had to get rich so I could sing like I was poor again.
—Dolly Parton[1]

Dolly Parton's career has become so multifaceted that it can be hard to remember that musical brilliance brought Parton to the national stage. So with that in mind, here's a completely nonexhaustive timeline of seven key moments in Dolly Parton's music career:

∼

1959   Parton, at thirteen years old, records "Puppy Love," her first commercially released record at Goldband Records in Lake Charles, Louisiana.

1974   After a successful seven-year run, including 218 television appearances and a dozen albums, Parton leaves *The Porter Wagoner Show* and embarks on a solo career. To commemorate the event she writes "I Will Always Love You."

1977   Parton goes pop and begins recording in Los Angeles instead of Nashville. In June an AP article says of her move to Los Angeles, "More than a few of the folks on Music Row are wondering out loud if their high steppin' friend might be letting herself in for a big fall."[2] That month she records "Here You Come Again," which reaches number 3 on the *Billboard* Hot 100, a pop chart.

1980   Parton stars in *9 to 5*, her feature film debut. The success of the film places her firmly within mainstream popular culture. Parton's theme song for the film reaches number 1 on the pop charts, and the success of the movie spawns a sitcom and later a Broadway show.

1986   Parton buys an interest in Silver Dollar City from the Herschend Family and creates Dollywood.

1998   Parton returns to traditional country music with a series of albums, beginning with *Hungry Again* (1998) and followed by a pair of bluegrass albums, *The Grass Is Blue* (1999) and *Little Sparrow* (2001). The last two albums become part of the bluegrass renaissance brought about in large part by T-Bone Burnett's soundtrack for the film *O Brother, Where Art Thou?*

2016   After the success of her *Pure and Simple* shows at Dollywood and the Ryman Auditorium in Nashville, Parton announces plans for a tour of the United States and Canada. With more than sixty dates it is her biggest North American tour in twenty-five years. The tour dates are announced two months after Parton's seventieth birthday. At the end of the year she premieres a new TV movie on NBC and raises millions to rebuild her hometown after wildfires burn down hundreds of homes.

~

Dolly Parton has the perfect country music background. Maybe only Loretta Lynn (the coal miner's daughter from Butcher Hollow, Kentucky) and possibly Merle Haggard (who as an inmate saw Johnny Cash perform in San Quentin) can compete—though Haggard ended up living in northern California, so I think Dolly probably has him beat. If you'll pardon the atrocious pun, Parton's life story hits all the right notes. From the park's two-room cabin to the cornbread and beans served at Dollywood, the place feels like a total immersion in the country lifestyle. The feeling is only confirmed when you go into her museum and see the walls of gold records, Grammys, and countless other awards that shimmer with the aura of country music superstardom.

It's all so perfect. It feels real and authentic, but it is a theme park—the most artificial kind of place you can imagine. So is the rest of it too perfect? Has Dolly Parton constructed a narrative for herself that she knows will sell? Has she written her life like one of her songs? Is the Dolly that we, the fans, see an artifice—and if it is, so what?

I'm not sure how to clearly differentiate Parton's public persona from Parton herself. This is not just because of my limitations; part of the strength of Parton's persona is that it feels so present, natural, honest, and real. So I ran into trouble when I decided to write about clarifying that persona. How do you differentiate between the public Parton and her private self? Both are who she is, both are real, and both matter. One is not more or less real; both are different facets of the same person. The public face is the one that concerns us as fans; it is also the one that relates directly to Dollywood and to her musical career—that is the one that matters here. She has kept her private self exquisitely private, most especially her fifty-year marriage to the reclusive Carl Dean.

Dean, and his reticence about being a public spouse, has been the subject of much curiosity and conjecture over the years. His private self probably qualifies as the greatest mystery about Parton.

To date little information about their marriage has become public. Parton says that her reclusive husband is uninterested in the trappings of fame but that both remain devoted to each other. In her autobiography she says that they don't see each other as often as most married couples, but for her the absence is what has kept their relationship strong. She describes snapshots of their life together that are sweet and, well, very normal—"I love to smell Carl's clothes. When we were first married I would smell that odor of grease and smoke (yes, he does smoke cigarettes, trying to quit). He leaves his work clothes hanging in the mudroom, and sometimes I'll just smell them, especially if he's not around, I'm going out of town, or I'm just missing him. Don't that sound silly?"[3]

In *In the Shadow of a Song,* her sister Willadeene describes Carl as popular with the family and pleasant to be around: "He is tolerant, open-minded, patient, sensitive. He has a sarcastic sense of humor, that all of us enjoy."[4]

So it would seem that Parton saves her marriage for herself and her husband. She has made (or they have made together) a deliberate decision not to be a celebrity couple that uses their private life to attract coverage.

On some of Parton's early work the copyright is listed as belonging to Dolly Parton Dean.[5] I thought this separated things nicely. So even though it feels a bit patriarchal, I'll use Dolly Dean in reference to the private person and Dolly Parton in reference to the public persona.

What interests me is that public persona. The private stuff remains a mystery, and I think it probably will for the foreseeable future. This is fine—we don't really need any inside information here. Parton's public work is such a part of the story that settling for the official doesn't actually feel like settling. Parton's authorized autobiography doesn't feel like antiseptic celebrity boilerplate. It feels like a great story.

I don't care to try to litigate Parton's persona, and if you're looking for insider gossip or a glance behind the curtain, I'm sorry to tell you I don't have any. I'm interested in what's in front of the curtain; I think Parton has given her fans plenty of herself in the form of her public self. Parton's persona is one of her creations. All told, it is her most important creation and likely her most enduring. She has crafted and evolved it over the years to create an iron-clad bond with her fans, who constitute one of the most ardent followings in all of popular music.

Before I look at how she has shaped that persona and how that creation has manifested itself at Dollywood, I want to make something clear. When I say that Parton has created her persona, I don't mean to imply any kind of value judgment. It doesn't mean that I think Parton is a phony, a pretender, or a liar. In fact, I think quite the opposite; I think Parton's persona seems to be a deeply personal one that holds a great deal of emotional honesty. That's why she has been so successful at connecting with fans. Parton's public image, Dolly Parton, is one of her creations, and creativity can be incredibly honest. But what she has given the public is carefully crafted, sculpted, and formed to provide a distinct idea of who exactly Dolly Dean wants us to believe Dolly Parton really is.

Since the 1978 biography *Dolly,* by Alanna Nash, Parton has declined to cooperate with biographers.[6] She prefers to tell her life story herself through her autobiography, songs, movies, and, of course, her theme park. It seems odd that someone who is such a great talker would seem to consent only to promotional interviews, but I think that Parton knows her strengths. She is a master of the quip—a skill that wins over every host and studio audience member, not to mention viewers at home. Repeated quips and retold stories don't go over as well with self-serious music reporters but are a perfectly reasonable defense mechanism. Biographers bring their own agendas and sometimes can have a regrettable tendency to get sloppy with the details other people's lives. They know that, to gain good sales, rather than recounting stories fans have heard before, they need to try to peel back Dolly Parton and get a voyeur's peek at Dolly Dean. I think it is more than fair that Parton's reward for her lifetime of discretion is the right to tell that story herself.

The other major factor here is trust. Dolly Parton has proved that she is a master storyteller; she knows that she can perfectly capture the essence of whatever part of her life she is trying to recall, whether on the page, on a recording, or on the screen. Why on earth would she give that power to someone else? After all, if we lose control of our own life, what do we have left?

The last factor, and what I believe is the most critical, is the importance of legend. Parton has spread her wings over almost every facet of popular culture, but she always has managed to maintain her country music credibility and legendary country values legend.

With the possible exception of the blues, country music has a stronger connection to place and personality than pop, rock, or even rap. Country music historically has had a unique relationship with its fans. This comes from the history of the music, which at times has been music for working-class people (or people who wanted that association) and sentimental music for people happy to be moved by country's often-melodramatic displays of sorrow, love, joy, and anger. That unique relationship has frayed over the years because of country's transformation to white suburban music—the mild replacement for rock 'n' roll as its sales have faded. Country fans want singers who project an image of country authenticity. Rural roots are helpful, so is the perception of a working-class background. A family history with the genre also helps, and a southern birthplace seems to be a big plus. No other genre is as obsessed with its stars' hometowns—and those hometowns never seem to be Cape Cod or the Upper East Side.

In his excellent biography of Dwight Yoakam, Don McCleese describes the importance of contrivance—a loaded term to be sure but one used here without any particular judgment: "What is show business—if not all of popular culture—but artifice that is essential to the art?" McCleese sees in Yoakam's fans what Samuel Coleridge termed "the willing suspension of disbelief." The idea is that we aren't being sold a false bill of goods against our wills. We want the creation because it makes the art more resonant to us. McCleese again: "Whether it is Hank Williams donning the cowboy hat that was never the fashion in his native Alabama, or Bruce Springsteen celebrating his working-class authenticity long after he became a bicoastal millionaire, or the lionization of the Clash playing revolutionary guerrillas backed by the promotional muscle of a mighty international conglomerate, we believe what we want to believe. What the art convinces us to believe."[7]

So it is with Yoakam, the embodiment of pure Kentucky country who happened to have been raised in Columbus, Ohio, and Dolly the hillbilly girl who can never leave the mountains yet is one of the music industry's most savvy business people.

To acknowledge the existence of a persona isn't an attack. It is simply an admission that we cannot truly know an artist. All we have is what they have given us, and Parton seems to have given us an awful lot.

$\sim$

When we talk about Parton's smarts or her business acumen, something that can get overlooked or at least undersold is that Dolly Parton is an important artist. I don't mean that she is important because she's written some good songs and had some crossover success. I mean that Dolly Parton is probably the most important artist in country music history. She's not the first to have been hugely important. That was probably the Carter Family or Jimmie Rodgers, followed by Hank Williams and probably Johnny Cash. Some folks will argue that others deserve votes, and that's fine. They all matter and all are important. But when was the last time you heard a country record that sounded like Jimmie Rodgers? Who is the last artist who played and wrote like Hank Williams instead of just talking about it? These artists have something else in common: they're mostly all men. In the vast landscape of twenty-first-century male country music, hardly any artists sound as though they've ever listened to Hank Williams, let alone the Carters or Rodgers.

For the first decade and a half of the twenty-first century, male country music has been far more influenced by classic rock, nu metal, and hip-hop than any of its artists would likely ever care to admit. The songs are mostly party anthems and ballads dedicated to confirming for their audience that a life filled with trucks, boats, daisy dukes, and small-town life is the real deal. Whatever the real deal is.

Peter Lewis analyzes the phenomenon in a post on *Medium* called "What Happened to Country Music?" In it he breaks down the lyrical themes of country songs from 1965 to 2015 and finds that in the sixties the vast majority of hit country songs were centered on themes like broken relationships and hard luck lives. In the millennial era he found those kinds of songs had completely fallen off the charts, replaced by songs about how love always works out and stories about the living the good life.[8] We've replaced poetry for commercials . . . and business has never been more profitable.

Lewis doesn't track how this evolution differs depending on the singer's gender, but luckily someone else did. In his sociology thesis, "Stand by Your Man, Redneck Woman," Cenate Pruitt finds that while the passage of time has provided a wider role for women in country, essentially similar trends were true for women and men. Where once heartbreak was a "nigh-crippling event that destroyed lives, now it is simply another obstacle to be overcome."[9]

I have a slightly different, if not wholly incompatible, theory. I think the men represented in country music today are afraid to appear broken in the way their forebears did, and I don't think this fear extends to country's women.

It is impossible to imagine the modern good ole bro walking the floor heartbroken the way that Ernest Tubb did or curling up at night and hoping that death will bring relief from loneliness as in the Hank Williams song. The chart toppers in today's country are too busy partying in the bed of a pickup truck or having a beer at the beach to notice their girl is gone. Much of modern country has become about proving to the rest of the world that the "country lifestyle" is superior to the way people live in cities or up North, or—I don't know—in Europe or someplace.

Blake Shelton shows you exactly what I'm talking about in his party anthem "Hillbilly Bone." It describes a New Yorker who doesn't know anything about southern culture. In fact, this city slicker has never heard of Conway Twitty (whose name happens to rhyme with New York City). Shelton's metropolitan friend is brought south for an education in "grits and greens." Shelton takes him honky-tonking, and the guy who had never been south of Queens takes to Shelton's idea of hillbilly life "like a pig to mud."[10]

See? The way Blake does it is better, y'all! Country used to mean hard times, now it means good times. What's interesting is that because women are still allowed to feel things like heartbreak and loss, they still sing relatively classic-sounding country songs.

Country music is at its most exciting when it is an unflinching portrait of the way people live. Romance, fantasy, and nostalgia run through country, certainly, but when country really clicks is when it *feels* real. For most of the genre's history it has never spoken more eloquently than when it has chronicled the life of poor or working-class America. Think of songs like Merle Haggard's "If We Make It through December," Loretta Lynn's "Coal Miner's Daughter," George Jones and Tammy Wynette's "Golden Ring," or Dolly Parton's "Hungry Again."

Have the good ole bros killed these kinds of songs? Have we traded heartbreak and hard times for beer cans in Koozies and good times at the lake house? I won't keep you in suspense: the answer is no—and the reason is Dolly Parton.

Women influenced and inspired by Parton still are making these kinds of songs. They still sing about real life. They create great songs about heartbreak, such as Miranda Lambert's "Mama's Broken Heart" (2013), or a lifetime of settling, like Pistol Annies' "Unhappily Married" (2013). They sing about running out of luck, as in Brandy Clark's "Get High" (2013) or Margo Price's "This Town Gets Around" (2016). They also cover ground that men never would—in "Pregnant at Prom" (2016) the Sevierville native Tara Thompson sings about—well—being pregnant at the prom. Another prime example is Ashley Monroe's heartbreaking song about the loss of sexual innocence, "The Morning After," which covers the painful and messy terrain of date rape from the consistently neglected perspective of a victim who isn't entirely sure that she is one. It is a complicated thing to write a song about, and complicated things aren't really all that common in modern country, especially the songs that get played on country radio.

In May 2015 an insider music business newsletter called *Country Aircheck Weekly* caused an Internet kerfuffle among artists, critics, and fans when it quoted a consultant on music scheduling, Keith Hill, who cautioned radio programmers not to give women artists a lot of air time on country stations. "If you want to make ratings in Country radio, take females out," Hill said, adding, "I've got about 40 music databases in front of me and the percentage of females in the one with the most is 19%. . . . Trust me, I play great female records and we've got some right now; they're just not the lettuce in our salad. The lettuce is Luke

Bryan and Blake Shelton, Keith Urban and artists like that. The tomatoes of our salad are the females."[11]

As Rob Harvilla, writing for the *Ringer*, pointed out, Hill inadvertently stumbled into a "a savage burn" when he equated country's leading men to a bowl filled with lettuce.[12]

In 2014 Kacey Musgraves took the stage at the Grammys and sang her song "Follow Your Arrow," which expresses support for recreational marijuana use and sexual exploration, and ambivalence about other people's opinions of same. Musgraves also performed the song a little more than a year later to celebrate marriage equality. If Musgraves's message of tolerance has an antecedent, it has to be Dolly Parton, who said in her 1994 autobiography—that's right: *1994*—that gay rights are human rights and that "I have many gay friends who I love dearly. I have also lost some very special friends to AIDS. I believe that being gay is something you are, not something you do."[13]

There is some historical precedent for this outspokenness. From the 1950s through the 1970s women quietly but assertively became country music's most interesting artists. In a genre often noted for its inherent conservatism and male dominance, the women who shaped country were countercultural by the virtue of their gender alone. This divide, and the uncompromising way that country's women went about asserting their identity, is perhaps best illustrated with the first song recorded by a female artist to become a number 1 hit on the *Billboard* country charts: "It Wasn't God Who Made Honky Tonk Angels" (1952), sung by Kitty Wells.

The song was written by producer Jay Miller in response to a song by Grand Ole Opry star Hank Thompson. In "The Wild Side of Life" Thompson tells of the perils of falling for a woman who'd rather spend time out on the town than making home for her man. In the chorus he says sarcastically to his wayward bride, "I didn't know God made honky tonk angels."

Wells rebutted Thompson's lyric with a powerful assertion of frustration: "Too many times married men think they're still single," she sings, explaining that cheating husbands are to blame for their good-hearted wives' wandering affection. This assertion dropped like a bomb into the country world of 1952. NBC Radio banned it outright for its suggestive nature, and the Opry told Wells she could not perform the song on its radio program. Despite these ham-fisted attempts at suppression, the Wells-Miller answer to "Wild Side of Life" outsold the original and became a smash hit.

"Kitty Wells was the first and only Queen of Country Music, no matter what they call the rest of us," Dolly Parton said when Wells died in 2012. "She was a great inspiration to me as well as every other female singer in the country music business."[14]

In her assertion of independence Parton went further than Wells. First Parton refused to settle for simply being Porter Wagoner's "girl singer," a term that reflects with grotesque precision exactly where women stood in the country landscape of the 1960s. Her profile rose as a result of her appearances on the show, but she felt constrained by working under someone else's name, even if that someone had a nationally syndicated TV show. Her departure from the variety show is chronicled in lyric form in her most famous composition, "I Will Always Love You." The song is one of biggest hits of all time, thanks in large part to a cover by Whitney Houston that is ranked as the seventh-best-selling song in history.

My favorite story about that song doesn't have anything to do with Whitney Houston's cover. It has to do with another stratospheric talent, Elvis Presley. I was talking with Jim Mills, an award-winning North Carolina banjo player who played on Parton's two bluegrass albums. I asked him about Parton, and he recalled she had once shared this story about the value of publishing: "Colonel Tom Parker, Elvis's manager, called Dolly and told her that 'Elvis wants to cut your song.' At the time, everyone knew that if Elvis did your song, you could be looking at millions. She had just started on her own and was elated. She said she just about jumped off the house. She went home and told all her family and friends, 'Elvis is gonna record my song!' She just couldn't believe it. Time went by and they were still in communication about the deal, and Colonel Tom Parker says, 'It's customary that anything that Elvis records, he gets half the publishing credit on.' And she said, 'I can't do it—I wrote that and it's my song.' And Parker said, 'Lady, are you crazy? Half the publishing credit on something Elvis does will make plenty of money.' But she said no. She said if she hadn't said no, she would have lost millions and millions—from that one decision."[15]

Parton has recalled in interviews that after she hung up the phone after that conversation with Parker, she cried all through the night.[16] Parton made a bold assertion of self to Parker. It would have been bold for anyone, but it was especially brave of a woman in an unfriendly business. Parton's demand that even the biggest machines in pop music respect her voice and her creative control has resonated through the decades and continues to empower country musicians today.

It's not to say that there is no hope for men in country music, but the possibility is worth examining. It is also worth pointing out that the women inspired by Parton, whether Lambert, Monroe, Musgraves, or many others, are unabashedly mainstream—or they would like to be. These aren't outlaws—like Willie Nelson or Waylon Jennings and their antecedents like Sturgill Simpson or Jason Isbell—who were working apart from the country music machine of Music Row. Dolly Parton's success has made it okay for women to make good work inside country's mainstream. You could even argue that Parton's pop music success during the *9 to 5* period laid the groundwork for later megastars, like her goddaughter Miley Cyrus, or Taylor Swift, one of the biggest entertainers in the world. Swift is by no means a country traditionalist like Monroe or Lambert, but she has built an international empire out of a beginning as a pop-country singer and songwriter from Nashville in an approach not dissimilar to Parton's forays into pop music in the 1970s and 1980s.

∼

A distinct element of the Dolly Parton persona that makes it so revolutionary is that she is unafraid to show us how smart she is. She is unembarrassed by her "white trash" roots and proud of her business acumen and considerable wealth.[17] Parton, I believe, feels that if she makes clear that she has made an empire not just with talent and luck but also grit and character, another young woman from the mountains might be inspired to follow Parton's advice to dream more and assert herself in life.

To accept this notion of Parton the public self as an empower-
ing feminist icon requires a bit of reconciliation. How do we square a
persona that at once says firmly and without equivocation, "I matter,
my voice is mine," with the character—the busty blonde mountain girl
with the Minnie Pearl one-liners? I think the answer to that requires
an embrace of that character—the caricature that causes a little quea-
siness in those of us in the business of criticism. Accepting it requires
an embrace of what might be dismissively called kitsch or camp—it
requires us to drop our ironic distance and allow ourselves to want to
actually be affected by culture.

The fundamental problem with kitsch is that it is, by its nature, distancing. Kitsch requires little buy-in. As the art critic Clement Greenberg writes in *Mass Culture,* "Kitsch pretends to demand nothing from
its consumers except their money—not even their time."[18] This lack
of connection means that kitsch is largely encountered as something
other people do and that is either observed or participated in with
some degree of ironic detachment.

Camp, like its cousin kitsch, builds walls between potential connec-
tions. However, unlike kitsch, camp is often self-imposed. The theorist
Susan Sontag defines camp as "the love of the unnatural: of artifice
and exaggeration."[19] It is an intentional distancing from reality, a mask.
That mask protects performers and audience members alike. Camp allows unspoken things to be said, because camp disguises itself as frivo-
lous, unimportant, and gauche. Camp creates a barrier, or a safe zone,
between persona and self. This gulf between artifice and identity is
what allows for the vulnerability of performance.

Some love kitsch and camp, but ultimately the audience has to be
in on the joke for any real connection to take place. Parton's style may
veer toward kitsch and her banter can certainly be campy, but these
impulses are just a veneer over a profound and genuine connection between her and her fans.

The error, I suppose, is to misunderstand the presence of kitsch.
To whatever extent it is present in Parton's work and embraced by her
fans, it is there by intention and not by lack of sophistication.

Compounding this problem is that observing kitsch and camp,
and commenting on their strangeness, is relatively easy work. As the

philosopher Theodor Adorno explains, "People want to have fun. A fully concentrated and conscious experience of art is possible only to those whose lives do not put such a strain on them that in their spare time they want relief from both boredom and effort simultaneously. The whole sphere of cheap commercial entertainment reflects this dual desire. It induces relaxation because it is patterned and pre-digested."[20]

The easiest thing to relay about Dollywood and Dolly Parton is camp. The first sentence of Kim Severson's 2105 *New York Times* piece on the park says, "At Dollywood, the place on a Venn diagram where gay camp and Southern camp overlap, cinnamon rolls might be the great equalizer."[21]

This kind of campy posturing is an easy and natural signifier for a place like Dollywood and a person like Parton. The cover of Helen Morales's 2014 account of her journey across Tennessee to the park features the book's title written in rhinestones and stretched like a T-shirt across disembodied breasts. Morales and Severson followed these hooks with thoughtful analyses and cogent observations. Ultimately even Rob Blackhurst, a correspondent for the *Financial Times* who harshly asked, "Is Dollywood one big kitsch joke?" finds the answer to be "not really," albeit through a thick helping of condescension. "For all its flag-waving, the full-throated celebration of southern life does capture something that is inspiring about America and goes beyond the God-and-guns clichés," Blackhurst writes.[22] Imagine if people had written with the same level of surprise that an animator had his own theme park. Disney was accepted as a businessman. When he opened his theme park, it became part of his business empire. It wasn't bizarre that a man who had brought a cartoon mouse to life by talking in falsetto was opening an amusement park—it was the shrewd maneuver of a seasoned businessman. To argue any differently about Dollywood would seem to be simply wrong-headed.

～

Because of their unabashed artificiality, theme parks are helpful places to examine social imaginaries. The British sociologist John Thompson finds that social imaginaries are the creative methods through which "human beings create their ways of living together and their ways of representing their collective life."[23] At theme parks these creative acts become the reifications of goals, aspirations, and ideals of those who wish to be removed from reality. Theme parks provide a wholly manufactured immersive environment that offers the experience of exposure to the desires, nostalgias, and imaginations of the creators and—when successful—the audience. Hyperreality, as Umberto Eco sees it, is the result of an audience's desire for the authentic reproduction: "The American imagination demands the real thing and, to attain it, must fabricate the absolute fake."[24] In Disneyland you can walk through a proxy of New Orleans's French Quarter without having to worry about the surprises, insecurity, and contradictions of the real thing. A theme park space is, after all, meticulously designed to be exactly what the visitor thinks it should be.

Dollywood presents a more complex example than Disneyland because Dollywood sits in the heart of the landscape that it represents. When you enter Dollywood, you leave Appalachia—a real landscape racked by the beauty, pain, ugliness, boredom, and extraordinary ordinariness that comes with a place lived in by real people. You enter what Eco would call the hyperreal. Dollywood is another Appalachia, as Dolly Parton and countless others imagine, remember, and wish it to be. It is more Appalachian than Appalachia could ever hope to be.

At Dollywood Appalachia is all cabins and homesteads, cinnamon bread, quilts, and banjo tunes. In the real world outside Dollywood's gates Appalachians might prefer heavy metal or live in prefab houses or avoid sweets. But inside Dollywood Appalachia is homespun and worry free.

Nostalgia is all about wanting the past to have been better; it doesn't have any connection to history—even though we like to tie the two together. This longing lies at the heart of Dollywood, where visitors can ride a log through a sawmill and eat pizza at a lumber camp in the Timber Canyon section of the park. This area depicts the dangerous workplaces of mines and mills as exciting and noble. In this imaginary Appalachian poverty doesn't pull you down—it builds you up.

When visitors to Dollywood are allowed to sense pain—for instance, the hardship of Parton's childhood at her coat of many colors display—the goal is to make you feel her eventual success and happiness even more acutely. We learn that Appalachian poverty also touched Dolly. In 1969 she recorded "In the Good Old Days (When Times Were Bad)." She grapples with nostalgia for the difficult history of the mountains. In the song she tells the listener that no riches would be worth trading in her memories, but she also cautions that you couldn't find a sum large enough to get her to live that life again.[25]

This sense of longing at Dollywood is tied to a uniquely southern imaginary. In their introduction to *American Cinema and the Southern Imaginary,* Deborah Barker and Kathryn McKee give an idea of what a southern imaginary might look like: "An amorphous and sometimes conflicting collection of images, ideas, attitudes, practices, linguistic accents, histories, and fantasies about a shifting geographic region and time."[26] With time these imaginaries can become a very real part of how people define themselves. Think of the power of these identifiers: Appalachian, Yankee, white trash, wealthy, southern. These once arbitrary distinctions become the essential building blocks of how people—or even places—are seen and how they see themselves.

Dollywood embraces these kinds of signifiers. It is a celebration of what Parton and her team imagine it means to be Appalachian. To physically enter an autobiography is a powerful moment and one that is unique. Tourists visiting Disneyland enter a physical manifestation of Walt Disney's imagination, but the implications of this fantasyland are different from an assertion of self. I don't think Disneyland is an autobiography. Dollywood is.

Dollywood is not just Dolly Parton's imagined South made real. It is the reification of myriad southern imaginaries. It reflects, confirms, and establishes countless ideas for its guests. It is also informed by countless images of Appalachia from people who have never set foot in Dollywood, or even the mountains that surround it, but who are informed through outside culture what Appalachia is supposed to look like. These people, who are on the outside looking in, conceptualize the region based on images of theme parks, Parton, and the myriad cultural signifiers of mountain life.

Dollywood sets out to move people, to connect with them. Dollywood, like Parton's music, goes unabashedly for the heart. That desire for emotional resonance complicates Dollywood. Critics seldom embrace affect and sentimentality, but both are beloved traits in country music. The contemporary cultural aesthetician Richard Shusterman argues that this desire for affect has distanced country culture from the academy: "Extreme emotion or sentimentality is a trademark of country music, and a prime reason why intellectuals dismiss it as vulgar kitsch."[27]

Dismissing Dollywood as kitsch is easy. The place is popular, designed for the masses, and requires only as much critical engagement as its audience is willing to give. Dollywood's primary goal is not to challenge or to question but to comfort and to entertain. Dollywood is calculated to appeal, but presuming that this makes the park somehow less substantial or reduces the meaning of the place would be a mistake.

This ability to sell a version of the South, even one that chafes at some sensibilities, is precisely why Dollywood matters. The South has a complicated history, as does the rest of the country—the rest of the world, for that matter. Selling history is also a complex act. What makes Dollywood work is that it doesn't pretend to give you history; instead it gives you something rarer—a chance to experience someone else's dreams. Whether you buy into those dreams and take them with you after you leave Parton's friendly confines is up to you.

These histories, philosophies, and imaginaries combine to create Dollywood. Looking at it from this perspective makes clear that Dollywood is a singular place, but strangely it is not singular. It makes perfect sense. A place like Dollywood could exist only in the Great Smoky Mountains, a region long informed by a tradition of selling local identity. How this theme park continues to develop speaks volumes about the evolution of mountain tourism in a region defined by marketing home and place. Dollywood could be presented with any kind of credibility only by Dolly Parton. Imagine Dollywood if it wasn't helmed by a woman who has been a pioneer, a progressive, an advocate, an evangelist, a hillbilly, a self-made millionaire, a genius, a wife, and an icon all without contradiction and without a hint of

insincerity. It would just be another place, another development trying to suck tourist dollars out of the Smokies. Dolly Parton makes the
place a site of education—a site of pilgrimage. Let me put it how I
know best: Dolly Parton is a damn boss.

Artifice, Celebrity, and Learning Something from Dollywood

Always remember that you cannot be more than a real somebody!
—Dolly Parton[1]

WE HAVE a tendency to view famous people as characters. We absorb them and fictionalize them. Of course, we also judge them.

I'm sitting in the lobby of the new Dollywood DreamMore Resort. It's March, so it's about as far as you can get from the height of the tourist season in Pigeon Forge. Dollywood is closed, and lots of places along the parkway are closed or have reduced hours. I thought I'd have the resort to myself, especially because the elaborate pool is closed for the cold weather, but I'm far from alone. Some kind of middle school cheerleading event and a songwriters' convention are happening, so the place is bustling. I'm killing time in a rocking chair near a giant portrait of Dolly and reading about Richard Simmons on my phone. Richard Simmons has me thinking about fame—and about Dolly's in particular.

The story is about how Simmons's friends and family are worried about him. The exercise guru–motivational speaker–sequence enthusiast has been reclusive lately. In fact, he's been in hiding.[2]

In the story we're told that his friends haven't seen him in years. He won't leave his home. Apparently his housekeeper prevents any contact with him at all. Plenty of famous people have opted for reclusiveness in their twilight years, but for Simmons it seems an uncomfortable fit. Simmons isn't particularly famous for any specific skill. His gift to the public is and has been his personality. He served as a motivator and jester for hundreds of people who were unhappy with their weight. This connection made Richard Simmons incredibly important to this group of people—even if it was impossible for the rest of the world to take him seriously. For Simmons's fans he was an inspiration, and that inspiration made him feel essential to their lives. Simmons, who by all accounts has a gentle and giving personality, reciprocated in kind.

The online comments about the article included stories about Simmons's meeting people who were trying to lose weight. Simmons would talk to them and, incredibly, would follow up by making calls of encouragement and tracking their progress. One blogger wrote in the *Huffington Post*, "I wrote to Richard Simmons many times. He wrote me back every time. It was the coolest thing ever. It amazed me how much he truly cared."[3]

A few days later, after I had returned from Pigeon Forge, Simmons released a statement and did a telephone interview with the *Today Show*. In it he said, "I just sort of wanted to be a little bit of a loner for a little while."[4]

I have my own theory about what has happened to Simmons. I think meaning so much to so many strangers was too much to take. Who knows what really went on in his life, but when he says he needed to be away from the world for a while, I kind of understand. People need Dolly Parton the way those people needed Richard Simmons. Like Simmons, every time Parton meets a fan, it is one of the highpoints of that person's life. Unlike Simmons, it appears, from the outside at least, that some of Parton's seemingly immense reservoir of energy comes from needing that need. I hesitate to call it an addiction—that seems grossly presumptuous—but I wonder whether Parton could stop. It seems strange to say, given Parton's success at keeping some parts of her life private—her marriage, for instance—but I find it impossible to imagine Dolly Parton as a full-time recluse. I suppose you never know. Perhaps one day she'll decide she needs a break and will cut herself off, get Carl Dean, and go to some ranch in Idaho to fall off the grid for a few years. I'd be surprised, though. Some people are just built differently—I think everyone knows that Dolly is.

~

I wasn't surprised when Parton graciously declined to talk with me about her park. I knew that she declines to speak with biographers.[5] She published an autobiography in 1994 and plans to publish a second volume in the near future. It seems that she intends these works to be the final word.[6] While some might position Parton's lack of interest in biographic journalism as somehow contrary to her open and honest public persona, it also stands to reason: the Dolly Parton persona is undoubtedly different from Dolly Dean, the person. It is important not to confuse the two here. That Parton has a manufactured public persona doesn't mean that her public image is fraudulent or dishonest. Parton's public face is a creative work, just like her songs and the theme park. Her biography, background, and demeanor are all part of her creative self and incredibly important to understanding her contributions. Think, for example of Mark Twain, Woody Guthrie, or Bob Dylan, all of whom understand that self-presentation is a critical piece of performance. Parton's ability to transmit a persona that is relatable, likable, and feels genuine and authentic is arguably as important to her achievements as her prodigious abilities as a businesswoman, movie star, or even as a songwriter.

Parton has earned tremendous success: two television shows (the 1976 and 1987 editions of *The Dolly Parton Show*) and Hollywood films, not to mention the thousands of songs she has written and recorded. Parton has earned more accolades and awards than any other female country performer. Her forty-six Grammy nominations are a record for a female artist. Parton continues to be the Smoky Mountains' favorite daughter. "This is my home—they have to be proud of me because I'm proud of them," Parton told Graham Norton, the British comedian and talk show host, for his 2001 special, *Graham Goes to Dollywood* for Britain's Channel 4.[7]

During every phase of Parton's career she has brought listeners back home in songs like "Coat of Many Colors," "In My Tennessee Mountain Home," "Hungry Again," and "Home." It seems natural she would eventually bring people to her physical home. Dolly Parton had a vision for this place. She wanted to create a permanent mountain theme park that captured the magic of the country fairs she had experienced as a girl. "You always got a day out of school to go to the fair. And, boy, that was the greatest day of my life," she recalled for *People* magazine. "I was fascinated with the freak shows. We'd crawl under the fence to look until somebody would kick us in the face to get us out. There was the spider woman who was supposed to have been found in the Amazon. Things like the fat lady. I patterned myself after her."[8] This carnivalesque personal construction put a curtain of kitsch around Parton's public identity while simultaneously endearing her to countless fans who felt like misfits and freaks in their home communities.

∼

Graceland. People have told me that I have to get to Graceland. They've told me Dollywood is like Graceland, an extension of our obsession with celebrity. I don't think they're right, although I can see why they make the connection. It is true, in some ways—especially geographically. Elvis's house and Dolly's hometown are Tennessee's musical tourist bookends. Both are icons dedicated to icons. But there, on the ground, they are so different. One of the biggest differences is a function of their locations: city versus mountains.

Memphis is a city in every sense. It is big. It is historic. It is diverse. It is complicated. It is part of the Deep South in a way that no other part of Tennessee truly is. Memphis, not Jackson, is the real capital of Mississippi—certainly of the Delta. Memphis is low topographically and dominated by the river. Planters and pickers shaped Memphis's history. It is impossible to imagine Elvis without Memphis, and it is impossible to imagine Memphis without Elvis. Graceland is a tomb. People who want to commemorate what has passed go there. The rest of Memphis's musical sites follow suit. Sun Records is a historic site, but mostly it's a gift shop and a cafe. Stax Records is now a foundation, school, and a museum. Beale Street still has live music, but even B. B. King's place is now a memorial. Other things tick on in Memphis: FedEx, ribs, and the eclectic mix of other cultural signifiers created in a big old city. More recently, Memphis became home to Bass Pro Shops at the Pyramid, a giant mirrored Egyptian pyramid originally built as an arena that now features a giant branch of the outdoor store and its archery range, bowling alley, and hotel. It is a decidedly odd mash-up of a landmark that would feel more at home on the Pigeon Forge Parkway than in downtown Memphis.

The biggest difference, what fundamentally separates Dollywood and Graceland, is that Elvis is dead, and his lack of life covers his house with a thick sense of loss and mourning. Dolly Parton is alive. Unlike Graceland, people don't go to her home to mourn the end of her life and the end of her creative output. They go to Pigeon Forge to receive one of her creations. Dollywood is a living, changing proposition, a piece of Parton's still vital empire and not a relic of what is left of her.

Dollywood also isn't real. Graceland was actually Presley's home. He lived there; his most private moments were there. Surely those moments ran the gamut: joy, pain, and finally fear. All free of the artifice of fame. If Elvis were still kicking, Graceland wouldn't be what it is today—because, assuming Elvis still lived there, it would be a home, not a shrine (and not Elvis's literal final resting place).

Dollywood doesn't have any private moments. The whole place is a performance. Theme parks and attractions with themes present their audiences with created environments. The pretend made real. In a theme park artifice is not problematic—the park's existence acknowledges that everything within its walls is fabricated. The immersive quality of the created environment is why guests are there in the first place. The whole place represents a mountain fantasy that is so pleasant and so honest in its falseness that any kind of search for authenticity has to be modified.

How does this work? How can a place be a total fabrication and authentic at the same time? First is this notion of honesty. Dollywood is a theme park, so we expect it to be like a stage set come to life. Second is the place. Whether park performers are from Sevierville or Staten Island, they are mountain performers because they perform in the mountains. They know the lines and songs, not out of some familial tradition but because they are professionals. Their job is to be mountain folk. Their job also is to sell the mountains in equal measure to everybody, no matter if they are locals or from far away. The other unspoken truth about theme parks, besides their artifice, is that no matter what ancillary benefits they might provide, they are places that exist first to make a profit.

Despite the corporatization of entertainment, there is real substance in the sharing of mountain life. The exchange can be from an insider to an outsider, but it is often a more knowing exchange from insider to insider. The stories, traditions, and even the stereotypes become identifiers of home. In *Homeplace,* Michael Ann Williams explains how narrative becomes an affirmative landmark in Appalachia: "The narratives I heard had been polished over the years, as people studied on their pasts and gave shape to their experiences. For the people who told them, the stories, too, were precious symbols of home."[9] Williams recounts narratives of Appalachian homesteads shaped largely by time, tradition, and nostalgia. Many of those same forces shape the narratives at Dollywood, but consumer culture also shapes these artifacts of place as commerce, tourism, and themed environments extend deep roots into the region and the identity of its people.

Dollywood has roots. They are there, even if they have slipped out of sight or been obfuscated by the constant drive to provide guests with something shiny and new. Its roots lie in the history of tourism in the mountain South and, more specifically, in Sevier County.

When people think about Dollywood, they usually describe it as an example of Parton's iconic status or another arm of Parton's financial empire. That is not an illegitimate angle, but it loses sight of the fundamental importance of what Parton has built in her hometown. The unique nature of transforming your childhood home, your biography, and your sense of place into a theme park is essential to understanding that place and to understanding Parton. Most important, treating Dollywood like another successful pop record or blockbuster movie, or even comparing it to Six Flags, ignores the deeper meaning of this place. Dollywood is a unique exercise in place making and biography.

To understand it as a mere corporate establishment disregards both the fundamental mission of the place and our powerful relationship and fascination with celebrity, aspiration, and myth.

Scholars who examine and explore themed environments have been quick to understand the significance of the artifice of places like Dollywood. In *Learning from Las Vegas* (1977), the architects and art historians Denise Scott Brown, Steven Izenour, and Robert Venturi argue that understanding illusion is critical to making sense of the cultural landscape. They embraced pop culture and the popularity of low-brow forms of culture consistently shunned by academic critique.

These destinations, like Disneyland, the Vegas Strip, or even road-side staples like Wall Drug in South Dakota or South of the Border in Dillon County, South Carolina, get pushed together and tossed into the kitsch wastebasket. To the extent that they are taken seriously, they are often filed away under "weird Americana," which seems to disregard how much these kinds of places must mean to people. If they don't matter on some level, why would people keep seeking them out?

Tourist traps also have a more reserved—but still manufactured—series of cousins: historic sites such as Colonial Williamsburg (Virginia, 1926), Connor Prairie (Indiana, 1934), and Greenfield Village (Michigan, 1929) are now accepted as cultural touchstones in American society. They operate under a veil of legitimacy brought about by their stated desire to try to re-create history. Educating the public is certainly a laudable goal, and a place like Williamsburg certainly does valuable historic work, but a visit to its website, which advertises spa packages and Busch Gardens tie-ins, reveals that perhaps it isn't so different from Dollywood after all. Dollywood wants to establish an Appalachian identity—however fanciful. Is that really so different from the noble origin story of colonial America told at Williamsburg?

In *The Themed Space,* a 2007 collection of essays about created tourist environments, Melissa Jane Hardie, an Australian academic who specializes in cultural studies, writes of Dollywood, "The park's purpose is to create an affective space where hearts are touched."[10]

Because of biases against kitsch, pop culture, or even southern accents, a place like Dollywood runs the risk of getting dismissed. It is naked in its ambition, both to entertain and to be a business. That sort of unambiguous nature rarely gets rewarded in cultural presentations. Often, the critics and cultural observers like ambiguity—and at Dolly-wood you have to look hard to find it. When a piece of culture is com-plex, its consumers can feel as though they've solved something, that they own a piece of the narrative. Rarely is a critically lauded piece of popular entertainment all that ambiguous, but that isn't really the point here. Nothing is ambiguous about a roller coaster designed to look like an eagle, or any roller coaster for that matter.

As I've already discussed, Dollywood is meant to be easy. At some level its survival as a business entity depends on its ability to be easily (and com-fortably) digested. That is why you find so many attractions and exhibits dripping with positivity and nostalgia. It follows, then, that you would ex-pect the hard questions about Appalachia to either be absent or obfuscated. For the most part this is true. Take the question of mountain poverty—for many it is a defining issue, one that is larger than politics. Is it discussed at Dollywood? I would argue that it is. Parton's life story is framed around growing up poor in the mountains. Her cabin, her coat of many colors, and her songs all speak to her personal experience dealing with lack.

Dollywood gently folds the issue of poverty into the theme park. It is mentioned only through the lens of Parton's personal experience. This approach allows a difficult subject to be subtly present without directly proselytizing in a way that might turn off some portions of the audience.

Dollywood is often presented as an unrefined place. In fact, Dolly-wood often presents itself as unrefined. It seems likely that it gets this from its namesake, who has summed up her sense of style by saying, "I have no taste and no style and nobody cares. I love it!"[11]

Parton obviously does have taste and she has style too. When she is saying that she doesn't have taste or style, she is really saying that she doesn't share the taste or style of her financial peers.

She's fond of describing her look as "a country girl's idea of glam." Parton likes to use this line in interviews and in her writings—even in her song "Backwoods Barbie," which is probably the song that best speaks to the issue of her self-presentation. In it she tells fans, "Don't judge me by the cover cause I'm a real good book."[12]

I don't think Parton is really saying that she's tacky. Instead what I hear when she says such things is that she is still one of us, that she hasn't gone above her raising and forgotten who she is and where her true people are. Of course, I'm not sure Parton was ever really one of us—how many of us are born to be stars?

Like Parton, Dollywood is also more refined than it gets credit for. It has honed itself and its presentation for decades, and Pigeon Forge has figured itself out over generations. So . . . what if we accept Dollywood's terms? What if we look at all the rhinestones and the chintz and just accept it as a fun coating on a carefully crafted experience? I understand that doing so feels like a risk.

We don't like to give in. I've argued here that Dollywood is a creative act. That makes it art. All art exerts its influence on us. I suppose that is why we are so guarded against art that seems to exist to separate us from our money. We know that art can take control of us. It can teach us, mold us, inform us, and move us.

Dollywood moves its audience by reflecting an imagined reality. The closest thing to what Parton has tried to do there is somehow allowing people to enter a dream—and selling tickets.

Helen Morales sums it up well: "Dollywood has its own temporal and spatial dynamics that were recognizable but nonetheless askew from those in everyday life."[13]

The remarkable thing about Dollywood is that, in synthesizing memories, nostalgias, and geographies, the theme park attempts to make ephemeral experiences into physical realities. The designers of the park do not attempt to create a spectacle of the bizarre kitsch—just the opposite; they hope to connect with their audience.

This ability to sell a version of the mountain South is precisely why Dollywood matters. The historian Karen L. Cox states, "For most of the last two centuries, one of the most valuable commodities the South has offered tourists has been its unique place in the history of the United States."[14] She describes iconic southern historic sites such as Mount Vernon, Monticello, antebellum mansions, Civil War battlefields, and steamboat cruises on the Mississippi, but she could just as easily include Sevier County, Tennessee, which has the most developed tourism industry of the five counties that host the Great Smoky Mountains National Park. Dollywood has so much resonance because of its connection to Parton's personal history and to the larger history of Appalachia tourism.

Dollywood is commercial and it is corporate. These are not simple things to be in the twenty-first century. They are even less simple to accept as a consumer or as a fan. I am certainly not advocating an embrace of corporate tourism; despite what commercials and agents would have you believe, it really is not for everyone. But, in the grand scheme of things, Parton seems to be a benevolent mountain overlord. She doesn't want only to expand her empire; she also seems to genuinely want to do right by her region and her people.

If nothing else, Dolly Parton represents a profoundly optimistic vision of what we can be. I want her America—I need it. I don't want the bullshit Dixie Stampede version; I want the real thing, the one that she has lived. I want to be from a country where a girl from a one-room cabin in Pigeon Forge can be the biggest star around. Where she can be the kind of person who doesn't make just her own dream come true but makes dreams come true for others. I want to live in a world where drag queens and evangelicals and evangelical drag queens have the same taste in music and sit side by side, singing at the top of their lungs.

I love Hank Williams, I love George Jones too, but I don't want their world. I want Dolly Parton's. I've spent a lot time talking about how Parton's biography is the ultimate country music origin story, but I think it is also important to remember that, for all the ways her story fits the genre's tropes, it is different in one big way: it is not a tragedy. Parton doesn't sell the self-destruction, sabotage, abuse, sorrow, and outlaw rage sold by so many of the other faces on country music's Rushmore. She hasn't drunk herself to death, popped pills, kicked out stage lights, beat up Carl Dean, or deserted her kids. She's never even done hard time. From the start of her career a huge part of her public image has been about the joy and beauty of seeing a spectacularly unusual, but still very human, being trying to be the world's most decent superstar.

This journey has created a phenomenal reservoir of both goodwill and a more general good feeling about Parton. This positive energy is what makes Dollywood make sense. If a little Dolly in your life feels good, why not try total immersion? Dollywood gives us a chance to experience her world.

At this point in the book, in theory, I should tell you some other side of the story, but I don't have another side. I don't have a dark side to show. I haven't met the person who has something bad to say or an axe to grind. I suppose I could gin up some cynical academic critiques of positivity and inclusiveness, but I don't have it in me to go after her. She hasn't earned that kind of attack. More important, I think that kind of attack would be dishonest—at least it would be if it came from me.

This is not just a matter of appreciating optimism. It's not only about accepting what Dollywood is selling. On some level I think it is immaterial to try to figure out whether people should or shouldn't y something—they clearly are accepting it and seem unlikely to stop. The question of why they buy it is important. Why do I buy it? This is personal question and the answer probably differs from other people's reasons. Maybe you like Dollywood because it presents a slightly surreal mountain fantasy, or maybe you like it because it has your favorite wooden roller coaster. I like the little room in the corner of Parton's museum where a video plays and people tell stories about Porter Wagoner. All these things are very Dollywood, and anyone who comes across them might love them—or not—for a wide variety of reasons.

Why we accept things can also be collective. I think Cracker Barrel restaurants are successful for many people because they simulate an experience that they miss or that they feel they've missed out on. Dollywood satisfies a need for its fans. The story of the park, in fact the story of tourism in Sevier County, is the history of that need.

We need to feel connected to nature. From the very beginning, people have been coming to the Smoky Mountains to do just that. Millions came as visitors, but some chose to stay and make the mountains their home. They built a life in the mountains, and those lives became fascinating to visitors. The crafts, songs, homes, and stories of the people who lived in the spectacular mountains became as much a part of the allure of the place as the curative springwater or picturesque views. We need stories for context, so we needed mountaineers to fill out the mountains. Whether Cherokee Indians, hillbilly moonshiners, or austere Baptists, the people of the mountains (real and imagined) filled in the place and made it palpable and exciting.

Those lives became stories and those stories became legends. The legends, even if they had a tendency to drift toward oversimplification and outright stereotype, were essential for visitors who came to the mountains. They became essential for many of the people who lived there too.

128 GONE DOLLYWOOD

This chapter's epigraph is from Parton's book *Dream More: Celebrate the Dreamer in You*. In it she exhorts her fans (or maybe her followers?) to follow their dreams. The last step in her plan is "be more."

"What does it mean to be more?" she asks. "Is it measured by how many hits I have or the number of awards that I've been given? Of course not." She explains that what she's after is something like the Golden Rule: "Be fair, generous and compassionate to everybody. And I do mean *everybody!* So if I have but one hope for you—always remember you cannot be more than a real somebody!"[15]

A real somebody. That's at the heart of Parton's message. It is at the heart of Dollywood. Dolly Parton is about self-fulfillment. She isn't about being cool—it's not that Parton isn't cool per se. She's extracool, above it. She presents things that most other artists might view as schmaltzy or trite.

Think of how separate Christian music is from mainstream pop music. This divide is perfectly evident at Dollywood—the Gospel Hall of Fame features dozens of artists who have sold countless records and draw huge crowds, but not more than one or two might register with even the most obsessive fan of secular music.

Parton is in fact a bridge between these worlds. On the back of the business cards of the Dollywood staff is a mission statement. It covers the basic hospitality points: exceed guest expectations, serve others, constantly improve, and so on. The last statement is written in boldface: "All in a Manner Consistent with Christian Values and Ethics."

The face of the company is Dolly Parton, who likes to tell a story about how she entered a drag competition as herself—and lost.[16]

Parton brings worlds together. That is a profound legacy, probably greater than any song or theme park. If you buy into Parton's fantasies—her lyrics, her persona, or her mountain wonderland—you buy into a small part of a dream. You share that dream with all her other fans. That means Christians, gays, liberals, conservatives, southerners, and people from all over the world are sharing a collective fantasy. That's the lesson of Dollywood. If Dolly Parton can pull it off, maybe the rest of us can get a little bit closer.

Maybe this message of togetherness sounds a little trite, especially when considering that it comes from a theme park. It makes sense to me, though, so if you don't want a piece of Dolly Parton's dream, you can go do your thing. I'll be at Dollywood.

A Note about Sources

A lot of sources were incredibly helpful in putting this narrative together. A comprehensive bibliography follows this note, but I'd like to
highlight a few sources that stand out as helpful further reading or that
were especially inspirational.

~

For history I relied heavily on C. Brenden Martin's *Tourism in the
Mountain South*. If you're interested in a broad view of how tourism
has shaped the entire region, I highly recommend it. For Sevier County
history Robbie D. Jones's *The Historic Architecture of Sevier County* is in-
dispensable. It not only contains a remarkable architectural survey of
the county but also begins with a nearly two-hundred-page chapter on
the history of the county.

I found Dolly Parton's own words to be the most helpful when
writing about her. I strongly recommend her 1994 autobiography,
Dolly: My Life and Other Unfinished Business. It is absolutely the first place
to start if you want to get a feel for Parton's story. If you want a real
treat, try to find the audio version, read by Dolly herself. It is criminally
no longer available, but copies of it show up online from time to time.
There are rumors she is considering a second volume of memoirs—I
hope she does it.

Steven Miller's unauthorized biography of Parton, *Smart Blonde*, is a
good start if you want an outsider's perspective. Also worth seeking out
is Alanna Nash's 1978 biography, *Dolly*, which takes a pretty deep dive into
who Parton was right before she became an international superstar.

Several great books on the mechanics of shaping identity in country music are available; particularly useful to me were Richard A. Peterson's *Creating Country Music* and Diane Pecknold's *The Selling Sound*. If you'd like to read a superb meditation on taste, take a look at Carl Wilson's *Let's Talk About Love: A Journey to the End of Taste*. It was originally published as part of a series, but he has expanded it into a stand-alone volume.

Last, I want to thank Mark Roberts, who made portions of his master's thesis, "Hillbilly Authentication," available to me. I'd also like to thank Susie Penman, who also made available her thesis, "Cracker Barrel's Culture: Exporting the South on America's Interstate Exit." Both are excellent and well worth tracking down if you'd like a deeper understanding of their respective subjects.

Notes

Chapter 1: Mountains, Parks, and Nothing Less Than Great

1. Dolly Parton, "Somebody's Everything," *Backwoods Barbie*, Dolly Records, 2008.

2. Dolly Parton, interview by Michael Munro, "Dollywood or Bust," *60 Minutes* (Australia), June 1986.

3. Steven Bridges, "Dolly Parton's Dollywood Apartment," Bridges Photography, 2011, http://sbphotos.com/dolly-partons-dollywood-apartment.

4. Tai Uhlmann, dir., *For the Love of Dolly.* Wolfe Video, San Jose, CA, 2008.

5. Associated Press, "New Resort at Dollywood on Track to Open This Summer," *New York Times,* February 12, 2015.

6. Hadley Freeman, "Dolly Parton: 'I May Look Fake but I'm Real Where It Counts,'" *Guardian,* August 21, 2011, http://www.theguardian.com/music/2011/aug/21/dolly-parton-country-music.

7. Pete Owens, interview by author, July 31, 2014, Pigeon Forge, TN.

8. James Rogers, "Fly Eagle Fly," 1973, http://www.friendsofjamesrogers.com/FlyEagleFly.htm.

9. Dolly Parton, *Dolly: My Life and Other Unfinished Business* (New York: HarperCollins, 1994), 133.

Chapter 2: Rebels, Tourists, and a Tennessee Mountain Home

1. Nancy Cardwell, *Iron Butterfly: The Words and Music of Dolly Parton* (Santa Barbara, CA: Praeger, 2011), 110.

2. Karl G. Heider, "The Rashomon Effect: When Ethnographers Disagree," *American Anthropologist*, New Series, 90, no. 1 (1988): 73–81, http://www.jstor.org/stable/678455.

3. If you are looking for a history of tourism in the mountains, you could do worse than starting with the work of C. Brenden Martin and David Whisnant, as the citations in this chapter show; I found their work to be tremendously helpful.

4. Steve Inskeep, *Jacksonland: President Andrew Jackson, Cherokee Chief John Ross, and a Great American Land Grab* (New York: Penguin, 2015), 238.

5. Frederick Hoxie, *This Indian Country: American Indian Activists and the Place They Made* (New York: Penguin, 2012), 52.

6. Louis Filler and Allen Guttmann, *The Removal of the Cherokee Nation: Manifest Destiny or National Dishonor?* (Malabar, FL: Krieger, 1962).

7. The land in Cherokee is not technically a reservation because the Cherokee purchased it from the federal government, but judging by the signage, *reservation* apparently has become an accepted term—or at least an easy shorthand for Indian land.

8. C. Brenden Martin, *Tourism in the Mountain South: A Double-Edged Sword* (Knoxville: University of Tennessee Press, 2007), 10.

9. Barbara Ballinger, "Foodie's Farm: Q&A with Blackberry Farm Owner Sam Beall," *Chicago Tribune*, June 12, 2013.

10. Martin, *Tourism in the Mountain South*, 18.

11. Lucy French, war journal entry, on June 22, 1863, Lucy Virginia French Papers, Tennessee State Library. Quoted in Martin, *Tourism*, 18.

12. Robbie D. Jones, *Historic Architecture of Sevier County, Tennessee* (Sevierville, TN: Smoky Mountain Historical Society, 1996), 31.

13. Ibid., 34.

14. Ibid., 71.

15. Ibid., 87.

16. Anne Mitchell Whisnant, *Super-Scenic Motorway: A Blue Ridge Parkway History* (Chapel Hill: University of North Carolina Press, 2006), 14.

17. Ibid., 23.

18. Richard Starnes, "Tourism, Landscape, and History in the Great Smoky Mountains National Park," in *Destination Dixie: Tourism and Southern History*, ed. Karen L. Cox (Gainesville: University Press of Florida, 2012), 268.

19. A. M. Whisnant, *Super-Scenic Motorway*, 32.

20. David E. Whisnant, *All That Is Native & Fine: The Politics of Culture in an American Region* (Chapel Hill: University of North Carolina Press, 1983).

21. Starnes, "Tourism," 280.

22. Martin, *Tourism in the Mountain South*, 128.

23. Jones, *Historic Architecture*, 153.

24. Martin, *Tourism in the Mountain South*, 131.

25. Ibid., 116.

26. Ibid., 159.

27. D. K. Wilgus, "Country-Western Music and the Urban Hillbilly," *Journal of American Folklore* 83, no. 328 (1970): 158.

28. Richard Smith, *Can't You Hear Me Callin': The Life of Bill Monroe, Father of Bluegrass* (Boston: Da Capo, 2000), 31.

29. Richard D. Starnes, *Creating the Land of the Sky: Tourism and Society in Western North Carolina* (Tuscaloosa: University of Alabama Press, 2005), 148.

30. Ibid., 146.

31. Jane S. Becker, *Selling Tradition: Appalachia and the Construction of an American Folk, 1930–1940* (Chapel Hill: University of North Carolina Press, 1998).

32. C. Brenden Martin, "Gatlinburg and Pigeon Forge," in *American Tourism: Constructing a National Tradition,* ed. J. Mark Souther and Nicholas Dagen Bloom (Chicago: Center for American Places, 2012), 112.

33. Becker, *Selling Tradition*, 73.

34. Elizabeth S. D. Engelhardt, "Creating Appalachian Women's Studies: Dancing Away from Granny and Elly May," in *Beyond Hill and Hollow: Original Readings in Appalachian Women's Studies* (Athens: Ohio University Press, 2005).

35. Becker, *Selling Tradition*, 42.

36. Jones, *Historic Architecture,* 6.

37. A walk in downtown Asheville, North Carolina, is immensely instructive in terms of thinking about the impact that the counterculture of the baby boomers had on the mountain South.

38. Helen Morales, *Pilgrimage to Dollywood: A Country Music Road Trip through Tennessee* (Chicago: University of Chicago Press, 2014), 112.

39. Joan Stack, "Whitewashing American History: A Review of Dolly Parton's Dixie Stampede," *Yesterday . . . and Today,* August 7, 2013, http://www.yandtblog.com/?p=1143.

40. Jones, *Historic Architecture,* 27–33.

41. Tim Tyson, interviewed on "Little War on the Prairie," episode 479 of *This American Life,* National Public Radio, November 23, 2012.

42. Morales, *Pilgrimage,* 117.

43. "Dolly Parton's Dixie Stampede in Pigeon Forge Gets New Look," WATE-TV (Knoxville), January 28, 2015.

44. Jones, *Historic Architecture,* 27.

45. U.S. Census Bureau. Percentages generated by author by using American FactFinder (factfinder.census.gov), March 2016.

46. "Modern Heros [*sic*]," Dixie Outfitters, Burlington, NC, http://www.dixieoutfittersnc.com/store/store_sub.cfm?Category_ID=2&Sub_Category_ID=146

47. Jack Hitt, "A Confederacy of Sauces," *New York Times,* August 26, 2001, http://www.nytimes.com/2001/08/26/magazine/a-confederacy-of-sauces.html.

48. Kristy Eppley Rupon, "2nd Generation at Maurice's BBQ Removes Confederate Flags, Avoids Politics," *The State* (Columbia, SC), October 25, 2013.

49. Kathleen Purvis, "Can a S.C. Barbecue Family Rise Above Their Father's History of Racism?" *Charlotte Observer,* December 8, 2016.

50. John Monk, "Barbecue Eatery Owner, Segregationist Maurice Bessinger Dies at 83," *The State,* February 24, 2014.

51. Horace Kephart, *Our Southern Highlanders* (Knoxville: University of Tennessee Press, 1913), 52.

52. Willadeene Parton, *In the Shadow of a Song* (New York: Bantam, 1985), 5.

53. Daniel S. Pierce, *Great Smokies: From Natural Habitat to National Park* (Knoxville: University of Tennessee Press, 2000), 166.

54. Julie Dodd, "Little Greenbrier School Provides Trip Back in History and Hiking Opportunities," Friends of the Smokies, June 11, 2014, http://friendsofthesmokies.org/blog/little-greenbrier-school-robin-goddard/.

55. Bonnie Trentham Myers, *The Walker Sisters: Sprited Women of the Smokies* (Maryville, TN: Myers and Myers, 2004), 93.

56. John Maloney, "Time Stood Still in the Smokies," *Saturday Evening Post,* 1946, http://www.saturdayeveningpost.com/wp-content/uploads/satevepost/time-stood-still-in-the-rockies-part-one-SEP.pdf.

57. National Park Service, nomination of "Walker Sisters' Place" for Inventory of National Register of Historic Places, prepared by Paul Gordon, March 16, 1976, http://focus.nps.gov/pdfhost/docs/NRHP/Text/76000169.pdf.

58. Martin, *Tourism in the Mountain South,* 53.

Chapter 3: Daisy Mae, Dreams, and Dolly

1. Stephen Miller, *Smart Blonde: Dolly Parton* (London: Omnibus Press, 2007), 225.

2. Barbara Walters, "Dolly Parton," *The Barbara Walters Special*, ABC. December 6, 1977.

3. Dolly Parton and Mac Davis, "White Limozeen" on the album *White Limozeen,* Columbia Records, 1989.

4. D. Parton, *Dolly*, 305.

5. David Allan Coe, Deborah L. Coe, and Fred Spears, "If That Ain't Country," on the album *Rides Again*, Columbia Records, 1977.

6. Bill Malone, *Don't Get Above Your Raisin'* (Urbana: University of Illinois Press, 2002), 86.

7. David Sanjek, "All the Memories Money Can Buy: Marketing Authenticity and Manufacturing Authorship," in *This Is Pop*, ed. Eric Weisbard (Cambridge, MA: Harvard University Press, 2004), 158.

8. Bill C. Malone, *Southern Music, American Music* (Lexington: University Press of Kentucky, 1979), 130.

9. Jennifer V. Cole, "Dolly Parton: The *Southern Living* Interview," *Southern Living,* September 11, 2014.

10. Dolly Parton, interview by Nate Berkus, *The Nate Berkus Show,* September 15, 2010, distributed by Sony Pictures Television.

11. Kitty Empire, "Well Hello Again, Dolly," *Guardian* (London), March 24, 2007, https://www.theguardian.com/music/2007/mar/25/popandrock.features2.

12. Huber Patrick, "The Riddle of the Horny Hillbilly," in *Dixie Emporium*, ed. Anthony Stanonis (Athens: University of Georgia Press, 2008), 78.

13. Harriet Beecher Stowe, *A Key to Uncle Tom's Cabin* (Leipzig: Bernhard Tauchnitz, 1853), 187.

14. Matt Wray, *Not Quite White: White Trash and the Boundaries of Whiteness* (Durham, NC: Duke University Press, 2006).

15. Daniel Harper, "Lobbyists Hold 'White Trash Reception' on Capitol Hill," *Weekly Standard,* July 9, 2012, http://www.weeklystandard.com/lobbyists-hold-white-trash-reception-capitol-hill/article/648303.

16. The Costume King, "White Trash," College Party Guru, http://collegepartyguru.com/themes/pages.php?link=White_Trash

17. *Barney Google and Snuffy Smith,* a comic strip created by the Chicagoan Billy DeBeck, was set in western North Carolina and debuted in 1919; it still runs today. *Li'l Abner,* by the Connecticut native Al Capp, was set in eastern Kentucky and first appeared in 1934, then ran until 1977.

18. Nathaniel Weyl, "The Geography of Stupidity in the U.S.A.," *Mankind Quarterly,* October 1974, 117–23.

19. Ibid., 119.

20. Bill O'Reilly, *The O'Reilly Factor,* Fox News, February 13, 2009.

21. Ibid.

22. Siobhan Lyons, "What 'Ruin Porn' Tells Us about Ruins—and Porn," CNN.com, May 16, 2016, http://www.cnn.com/2015/10/12/architecture /what-ruin-porn-tells-us-about-ruins-and-porn/.

23. The Marketing Arm, http://www.themarketingarm.com/capabilities /celebrity-talent/.

24. Duff McDonald, "The Celebrity Trust Index," *New York,* March 6, 2006.

25. Dolly Parton, *Dolly: My Life and Other Unfinished Business* (New York: HarperCollins, 1994), 42.

26. Ibid., 38.

27. Chet Flippo, "Interview: Dolly Parton," *Rolling Stone,* August 25, 1977, http://www.rollingstone.com/music/features/dolly-parton-19770825.

28. Nellie Andreeva, "NBC Developing Dolly Parton TV Movies," *Deadline: Hollywood,* January 16, 2016.

29. Steven Herek, dir., *Coat of Many Colors* (Burbank, CA: Warner Bros. Television, 2015), DVD.

30. D. Parton, *Dolly,* 124.

31. Dolly Parton, "Coat of Many Colors," RCA Records, 1971; Nancy Cardwell, *Iron Butterfly: The Words and Music of Dolly Parton* (Santa Barbara, CA: Praeger, 2011), 9.

32. Mark Allen Roberts, "Hillbilly Authentication: Investigating Authentic Regional Identity in Postmodern Appalachian Culture," master's thesis, Union Institute and University, Cincinnati, 2007, 34.

33. Ibid., 37.

34. Jason Fishman points out that although "many people assume the Dollywood trains were custom built for the theme park, the locomotives were actually constructed in the late 1930s and early 1940s," and that during World War II, "these steam engines played an important role in America's war effort," hauling freight on the White Pass and Yukon Route between the port of Skagway, Alaska, and Whitehorse, in Canada's Yukon Territory, for the construction of the Alaska Highway. Fishman, "The Secret History of the Dollywood Trains during WWII," *Visit My Smokies,* http:// www.visitmysmokies.com/blog/pigeon-forge/attractions-pigeon-forge /secret-history-of-dollywood-trains-during-wwii/, November 20, 2016.

35. Allen Eaton, *Handicrafts of the Southern Highlands* (1937; reprint, New York: Dover, 1973).

36. David Van Dommelen, *Allen H. Eaton: Dean of American Crafts* (Pittsburgh: Local History, 2004).

37. Eaton, *Handicrafts*, 4, 22.

38. Tim Hollis, *The Land of the Smokies* (Jackson: University Press of Mississippi, 2007), 132.

39. Martin, *Tourism in the Mountain South*, 59.

40. Abram Brown, "The Wild Ride of the Herschends: When Amusement Parks Are the Family Business," *Forbes*, May 7, 2014, https://www.forbes.com/sites/abrambrown/2014/05/07/the-wild-ride-of-the-herschends-when-amusement-parks-are-the-family-business/#5cb3cef17022.

41. Ibid.

42. Martin, *Tourism in the Mountain South*, 131.

43. Brown, "Wild Ride."

44. D. Parton, *Dream More*, 73.

45. Laura Bly, "Hooray for Dollywood: Tennessee Theme Park Celebrates 25th Anniversary," *USA Today*, May 25, 2010.

46. Miller, *Smart Blonde*, 225.

47. Ibid., 224.

48. Morales, *Pilgrimage*, 119.

49. John Gerome, "Dolly Parton's Book-Giving Charity: You Can Read a Lot into It," *Washington Post*, January 22, 2006.

50. Don Jacobs and Steve Ahillen, "Mayor: Gatlinburg Wildfires Caused $500M in Damages," *Knoxville News-Sentinel*, December 28, 2016.

51. Kat Kinsman, "After the Gatlinburg Fire, a Cast-Iron Maker and Dolly Parton Step Up to Help," *Extra Crispy*, December 13, 2016; "Over $100,000 Raised for Families Affected by Wildfires," press release, Lodge Cast Iron, December 22, 2016, http://www.lodgemfg.com/story/great-smoky-mountains-skillet-helps-families-affected-by-tn-wildfires.

Chapter 4: Pancakes, Paula Deen, and the Pigeon Forge Parkway

1. Lina Das, "'I've Got Used to People Looking at Them, Don't You Worry': Dolly Parton Gets Up Front and Very Personal," *Daily Mail*, February 5, 2010, http://www.dailymail.co.uk/tvshowbiz/article-1248658/Dolly-Parton-personal.html.

2. Titanic Pigeon Forge, "About Titanic," http://www.titanicpigeonforge.com/about/about-titanic (accessed July 20, 2015).

3. Pigeon Forge Department of Tourism, "Dolly Parton's Smoky Mountain Adventures," http://www.mypigeonforge.com/business/dolly-partons-smoky-mountain-adventures/.

4. Doc Collier Moonshine, http://www.doccollier.com (accessed July 25, 2015); Sugarlands Distilling Company, http://www.sugarlandsdistilling. com (accessed July 25, 2015); Ole Smoky Distillery, "Our Heritage," http://olesmoky.com/about/history (accessed July 25, 2015).

5. "Hard Rock Cafe Pigeon Forge Is Now Open," *WBIR*, www.wbir. com/story/news/local/sevierville-sevier/2014/05/14/hard-rock-cafe -pigeon-forge-to-open-next-week/9096443/ (accessed February 19, 2015); Kyle Grainger, "Margaritaville Opens New Hotel in Pigeon Forge," *Local8Now .com*, October 10, 2014, http://www.local8now.com/home/headlines /Margaritaville-opens-new-hotel-in-Pigeon-Forge--278846441.html (accessed May 31, 2017).

6. Kim Severson, "Paula Deen's Cook Tells of Slights, Steeped in History," *New York Times,* June 24, 2013; Alan Blinder, "Racial Bias Claim Dismissed for Paula Deen," *New York Times,* August 12, 2013.

7. Kim Severson, "Paula Deen Loses Major Endorsement Deal," *New York Times,* June 24, 2013; Hillary Dixler, "Paula Deen Is Opening a New Restaurant in Tennessee," *Eater,* February 26, 2014, www.eater.com/2014/2/26/6273137/ paula-deen-is-opening-a-new-restaurant-in-tennessee.

8. Glenn Smith, Melissa Boughton, and Robert Behre, "Nine Dead after 'Hate Crime' Shooting at Emanuel AME," *Post and Courier* (Charleston, SC), June 17, 2015.

9. Richard Fausset and Alan Blinder, "Era Ends as South Carolina Lowers Confederate Flag," *New York Times,* July 10, 2015.

10. Sadie Gennis, "A Timeline of Paula Deen's Downfall," *TV Guide,* June 27, 2013; Paula Forbes, "Caesars Terminates Relationship with Paula Deen, Shutters Four Restaurants," *Eater,* June 26, 2013, www.eater.com/2013/6/26/6414127 /caesars-terminates-relationship-with-paula-deen-shutters-four.

11. Michael Twitty, "An Open Letter to Paula Deen," *Afroculinaria,* June 25, 2013, www.afroculinaria.com/2013/06/25/an-open-letter-to-paula-deen/.

12. In the 1930s Coal Creek changed its name to Lake City after the completion of a nearby Tennessee Valley Authority dam formed an artificial lake. In 2014, in an effort to attract tourist development, the town again changed its name, this time to Rocky Top after Felice and Boudleaux Bryant's hit song, despite objections from the songwriters' estate. Associated Press, "Tennessee Town Changes Name to 'Rocky Top' in Bid to Attract Tourists," June 26, 2014, http://www.foxnews.com/us/2014/06/26/tennessee -town-changes-name-to-rocky-top-in-bid-to-attract-tourists.html.

13. Jones, *Historic Architecture,* 86.

14. Martin, *Tourism in the Mountain South*, 110.

15. Appalachian Regional Commission, "Tourism Development," n.d., www.arc.gov/tourism (accessed July 30, 2015); Appalachian Regional Commission and National Geographic, "Geotourism MapGuide to Appalachia: Featured Sites," https://www.arc.gov/mapguide (accessed August 1, 2015).

16. Martin, *Tourism in the Mountain South*, 107.

17. Gail Crutchfield, "Pancake Pantry Celebrating 50 Years in Business," *Mountain Press*, March 24, 2010, http://mountainpress.uber.matchbin.net/printer_friendly/6700080.

18. Joe Edwards, "Pancake House Has Been Serving Smoky Mountains Visitors for 50 Years," *USA Today*, March 10, 2010.

19. Leon Downey, telephone interview by author, July 31, 2014.

20. Tim Berry, interview by author, July 31, 2014, Pigeon Forge, TN.

Chapter 5: Okra, Chicken Livers, and a Break for Dinner

1. Dolly Parton, "Dolly Parton Celebrates Gold with Cracker Barrel," YouTube, August 27, 2012, https://www.youtube.com/watch?v=mIlTd9mfvgM.

2. John Egerton, *The Americanization of Dixie: The Southernization of America* (New York: Harper's Magazine Press, 1974).

3. Tammy Ingram, *Dixie Highway: Road Building and the Making of the Modern South, 1900–1930* (Chapel Hill: University of North Carolina Press, 2014), 2.

4. "Dan Evins," Cracker Barrel, n.d., https://www.crackerbarrel.com/about/newsroom/fact-sheets/dan-evins.

5. Ibid.

6. Susie Penman, "Cracker Barrel's Culture: Exporting the South on America's Interstate Exits," master's thesis, University of Mississippi, 2012, 10.

7. Cracker Barrel, "Get to Know Us," https://www.crackerbarrel.com/newsroom/media-kit/background (accessed October 31, 2017).

8. Michael Beverland, *Building Brand Authenticity: 7 Habits of Iconic Brands* (New York: Palgrave Macmillan, 2009), 33.

9. Amanda Petrusich, *It Still Moves: Lost Songs, Lost Highways, and the Search for the Next American Music* (New York: Faber and Faber, 2008), 177.

10. Emily Langer, "Dan Evins, founder of Cracker Barrel Highway Empire, Dies," *Washington Post*, January 16, 2012, http://www.washingtonpost.com/local/obituaries/dan-evins-founder-of-cracker-barrel-highway-empire-dies/2012/01/16/gIQAfkt43P_story.htm.

11. Don Steinburg, "Cracker Barrel: The Starbucks of Country Music," *Wall Street Journal,* August 1, 2013.

12. Douglas Martin, "Danny Evins, Restaurant Founder and Focus of Controversy, Dies at 76," *New York Times,* January 16, 2012.

13. Ibid.

14. Jake Tapper, "Cracker Barrel May Face Another Lawsuit," *ABC News,* October 17, 2006, http://abcnews.go.com/US/LegalCenter/story?id=2577627.

15. David Wasserman, "Will the 2012 Election be a Contest of Whole Foods vs. Cracker Barrel Shoppers?," *Washington Post,* December 9, 2011, http://www.washingtonpost.com/opinions/will-the-2012-election-be-a-contest-of-whole-foods-vs-cracker-barrel-shoppers/2011/09/28/gIQAMuXDiO_story.html.

16. Drew Magary, "Duck Dynasty's Phil Robertson Gives Drew Magary a Tour," *GQ,* January 2014.

17. Corienne Lestch, "'Duck Dynasty' Fans Given Scripted Apology by Cracker Barrel After Abrupt Reversal of Pulled Merchandise," *New York Daily News,* December 26, 2013.

18. Wayne Bledsoe, "Dolly Parton Responds to Dollywood Splash Country T-Shirt Controversy," *Knoxville News Sentinel,* August 2, 2011.

19. Kim Severson, "Dollywood: A Little Bit Country, a Little Bit Gay," *New York Times,* August 22, 2014.

20. Charles Wilson Reagan, interview by Sara C. Milam, "A Helping of Gravy: Southern Food and Pop Culture," *Gravy,* November 21, 2014, reprinted by Southern Foodways Alliance, February 10, 2015, http://www.southernfoodways.org (accessed February 11, 2015).

21. Jia Tolentino, "Letter of Recommendation: Cracker Barrel," *New York Times,* January 28, 2016.

Chapter 6: Biography, Persona, and Reality

1. Dolly Parton, *Dream More* (New York: Putnam, 2012), 108.

2. Associated Press, "Dolly: Parton Goes Pop," *Observer-Reporter* (Washington, PA), June 29, 1977.

3. Dolly Parton, *Dolly: My Life and Other Unfinished Business* (New York: HarperCollins, 1994), 153.

4. Willadeene Parton, *In the Shadow of a Song* (New York: Bantam, 1985), 143.

5. One example is *The Dolly Parton Scrapbook,* an authorized photo-bio published in 1978.

6. Alanna Nash, *Dolly* (Los Angeles: Reed Books, 1978).

7. Don McCleese, *Dwight Yoakam: A Thousand Miles From Nowhere* (Austin: University of Texas Press, 2012), 83. Coleridge coined the phrase in 1817's *Biographia Literaria,* http://www.english.upenn.edu/~mgamer/Etexts/biographia.html.

8. Peter Lewis, "What Happened to Country Music," *Medium,* April 30, 2016, https://medium.com/@plewis67/what-happened-to-country-music-300cf8303430#.ejr7fokak.

9. Cenate Pruitt, "Stand by Your Man, Redneck Woman: Towards a Historical View of Country Music Gender Roles," master's thesis, Georgia State University, 2006, 66.

10. Luke Laird and Craig Wiseman, "Hillbilly Bone," Universal Music, 2010.

11. Russ Penuell, "On Music and Scheduling," *Country Aircheck Weekly,* May 26, 2015, 8, www.countryaircheck.com/pdf_publication/Issue_449 - May 26, 2015.pdf.

12. Rob Harvilla, "Country Music Can't Hide behind Chris Stapleton Forever," *Ringer,* June 13, 2016, theringer.com.

13. Hollie McKay, "Kacey Musgraves' 'Follow Your Arrow' Latest Sign of Shifts in Country Music," *Fox News,* February 7, 2014, http://www.foxnews.com/entertainment/2014/02/07/kacey-musgraves-follow-your-arrow-latest-sign-shifts-in-country-music.html; Madeline Roth, "Watch Kacey Musgraves Sing 'Follow Your Arrow' for Marriage Equality," *MTV,* June 26, 2015, http://www.mtv.com/news/2198271/kacey-musgraves-follow-your-arrow-marriage-equality/; D. Parton, *Dolly,* 309.

14. Alan Duke, "Kitty Wells Blazed Country Path for Women," *CNN.com,* July 17, 2012, http://www.cnn.com/2012/07/17/showbiz/kitty-wells-legacy/.

15. Jim Mills, personal communication, 2015.

16. CMT.com staff, "Dolly Parton Reflects on Her Greatest Moments," *CMT News,* July 7, 2006, http://www.cmt.com/news/1535871/dolly-parton-reflects-on-her-greatest-moments/.

17. Stephanie Robbins, "Dolly Parton Is Proud of Being 'White Trash,'" *People,* September 11, 2014.

18. Clement Greenberg, "Avant-Garde and Kitsch," in *Mass Culture: The Popular Arts in America,* ed. Bernard Rosenberg and David Manning White (Glencoe, IL: Free Press, 1957), 102.

19. Susan Sontag, "Notes on Camp," in *Against Interpretation* (New York: Picador, 1964), 275.

20. Theodor Adorno, "On Popular Music," *Studies in Philosophy and Social Science* 9 (1941): 38.

21. Kim Severson, "Dollywood: A Little Bit Country, a Little Bit Gay," *New York Times,* August 22, 2014.

22. Helen Morales, *Pilgrimage to Dollywood: A Country Music Road Trip through Tennessee* (Chicago: University of Chicago Press, 2014); Rob Blackhurst, "Is Dollywood One Big Kitsch Joke?" *Financial Times,* July 11, 2009.

23. John B. Thompson, *Studies in the Theory of Ideology* (Berkeley: University of California Press, 1984), 6.

24. Umberto Eco, "Travels in Hyperreality," in *Travels in Hyperreality: Essays* (San Diego: Harcourt Brace Jovanovich, 1986), 8.

25. Dolly Parton, "In the Good Old Days (When Times Were Bad)," on the album *In the Good Old Days (When Times Were Bad),* RCA Nashville, 1969.

26. Deborah Barker and Kathryn McKee, introduction to *American Cinema and the Southern Imaginary* (Athens: University of Georgia Press, 2011), 2.

27. Richard Shusterman, "Moving Truth: Affect and Authenticity in Country Musicals" *Journal of Aesthetics and Art Criticism* 57, no. 2 (Spring 1999): 226.

Chapter 7: Artifice, Celebrity, and Learning Something from Dollywood

1. Dolly Parton, *Dream More* (New York: Putnam, 2012), 95.

2. Andy Martino, "Where's Richard Simmons?" *New York Daily News,* March 12, 2016.

3. Tony Posnanski, "An Ode to Richard Simmons," *The Blog, Huffington Post,* January 9, 2014, http://www.huffingtonpost.com/tony-posnanski/richard-simmons_b_4459874.html.

4. Charles Bramesco, "The Sad, Strange Plight of Richard Simmons May Have Finally Been Revealed," *Vanity Fair,* March 12, 2016.

5. Stephen Miller, *Smart Blonde: Dolly Parton* (London: Omnibus, 2007), ix; and Nancy Cardwell, *Iron Butterfly: The Words and Music of Dolly Parton* (Santa Barbara, CA: Praeger, 2011), 4.

6. Dolly Parton, *Dolly: My Life and Other Unfinished Business* (New York: HarperCollins, 1994).

7. Jon Magnusson, dir., *Graham Goes to Dollywood,* television special, December 16, 2002, for Channel 4 (UK).

8. Scott Haller, "Dolly Parton: Come on Down to Dollywood," *People,* May 5, 1986.

9. Michael Ann Williams, *Homeplace* (Charlottesville: University of Virginia Press, 1991), 136.

10. Melissa Jane Hardie, "Torque: Dollywood, Pigeon Forge, and Authentic Feeling in the Smoky Mountains," in *The Themed Space,* ed. Scott A. Lukas (Lanham, MD: Lexington, 2007), 23.

11. D. Parton, *Dream More,* 105.

12. Dolly Parton, "Backwoods Barbie," Dolly Records, 2008.

13. Helen Morales, *Pilgrimage to Dollywood: A Country Music Road Trip through Tennessee* (Chicago: University of Chicago Press, 2014), 121.

14. Karen L. Cox, introduction to *Destination Dixie: Tourism and Southern History,* ed. Cox (Gainesville: University Press of Florida, 2012), 1.

15. D. Parton, *Dream More,* 95.

16. Ibid., 91.

Bibliography

Adorno, Theodor. "On Popular Music." *Studies in Philosophy and Social Science* 9 (1941): 17–48.

Barker, Deborah E., and Kathryn McKee. Introduction to *American Cinema and the Southern Imaginary*, edited by Deborah E. Barker and Kathryn McKee, 1–26. Athens: University of Georgia Press, 2011.

Bauman, Richard, Patricia Sawin, and Inta Gale Carpenter. *Reflections on the Folklife Festival: An Ethnography of Participant Experience*. Bloomington: Folklore Institute, Indiana University, 1992.

Becker, Jane S. *Selling Tradition: Appalachia and the Construction of an American Folk, 1930–1940*. Chapel Hill: University of North Carolina Press, 1998.

Berman, Connie. *The Dolly Parton Scrapbook*. New York: Grosset & Dunlap, 1978.

Beverland, Michael. *Building Brand Authenticity: 7 Habits of Iconic Brands*. New York: Palgrave Macmillan, 2009.

Cardwell, Nancy. *Iron Butterfly: The Words and Music of Dolly Parton*. Santa Barbara, CA: Praeger, 2011.

Ching, Barbara. *Wrong's What I Do Best*. New York: Oxford University Press, 2001.

Cobb, James C. *Redefining Southern Culture: Mind and Identity in the Modern South*. Athens: University of Georgia Press, 1999.

Daugneaux, Christine B. *Appalachia: A Separate Place, A Unique People*. Parsons, WV: McClain, 1981.

Doss, Erika. *Elvis Culture: Fans, Faith, & Image*. Lawrence: University Press of Kansas, 1999.

Dykeman, Wilma. *The French Broad*. New York: Holt, Rinehart and Winston, 1974.

Eaton, Allen. *Handicrafts of the Southern Highlands*. 1937. Reprint, New York: Dover, 1973.

Eco, Umberto. "Travels in Hyperreality." In *Travels in Hyperreality: Essays.* San Diego: Harcourt Brace Jovanovich, 1986.

Edge, John T., ed. *The New Enclyclopedia of Southern Culture: Foodways.* Chapel Hill: University of North Carolina Press, 2007.

Engelhardt, Elizabeth S. D. "Creating Appalachian Women's Studies: Dancing Away from Granny and Elly May." In *Beyond Hill and Hollow: Original Readings in Appalachian Women's Studies,* edited by Elizabeth S. D. Engelhardt, 1–19. Athens: Ohio University Press, 2005.

———. *A Mess of Greens.* Athens: University of Georgia Press, 2011.

Filler, Louis, and Allen Guttmann. *The Removal of the Cherokee Nation: Manifest Destiny or National Dishonor?* Malabar, FL: Krieger, 1962.

Fox, Aaron A. *Real Country: Music and Language in Working-Class Culture.* Durham, NC: Duke University Press, 2004.

Greenberg, Clement. "Avant-Garde and Kitsch." In *Mass Culture: The Popular Arts in America,* edited by Bernard Rosenberg and David Manning White, 98–107. Glencoe, IL: Free Press, 1957.

Hardie, Melissa Jane. "Torque: Dollywood, Pigeon Forge, and Authentic Feeling in the Smoky Mountains." In *The Themed Space,* edited by Scott A. Lukas, 23–37. Lanham, MD: Lexington, 2007.

Herek, Steven, dir. *Coat of Many Colors.* Burbank, CA: Warner Bros. Television, 2015. DVD.

Hollis, Tim. *Dixie before Disney: 100 Years of Roadside Fun.* Jackson: University Press of Mississippi, 1999.

———. *The Land of the Smokies.* Jackson: University Press of Mississippi, 2007.

Hoxie, Frederick. *This Indian Country: American Indian Activists and the Place They Made.* New York: Penguin, 2012.

Huber, Patrick. "The Riddle of the Horny Hillbilly." In *Dixie Emporium: Tourism, Foodways, and Consumer Culture in the American South,* edited by Anthony J. Stanonis, 69–86. Athens: University of Georgia Press, 2008.

Ingram, Tammy. *Dixie Highway: Road Building and the Making of the Modern South, 1900–1930.* Chapel Hill: University of North Carolina Press, 2014.

Inskeep, Steve. *Jacksonland: President Andrew Jackson, Cherokee Chief John Ross, and a Great American Land Grab.* New York: Penguin, 2015.

James, Otis. *Dolly Parton.* New York: Jove, 1978.

Jones, Robbie D. *Historic Architecture of Sevier County, Tennessee.* Sevierville, TN: Smoky Mountain Historical Society, 1996.

Kephart, Horace. *Our Southern Highlanders.* Knoxville: University of Tennessee Press, 1913.

Lowenthal, David. *The Past Is a Foreign Country*. Cambridge: Cambridge University Press, 1985.

Magnusson, Jon, dir. *Graham Goes to Dollywood*. Television special. Channel 4 (UK). December 16, 2002.

Malone, Bill. *Don't Get Above Your Raisin'*. Urbana: University of Illinois Press, 2002.

Martin, C. Brenden. "Gatlinburg and Pigeon Forge, Tennessee." In *American Tourism: Constructing a National Tradition*, edited by J. Mark Souther and Nicholas Dagen Bloom, 111–18. Chicago: Center for American Places, 2012.

———. *Tourism in the Mountain South: A Double-Edged Sword*. Knoxville: University of Tennessee Press, 2007.

McCleese, Don. *Dwight Yoakam: A Thousand Miles from Nowhere*. Austin: University of Texas Press, 2012.

Miller, Stephen. *Smart Blonde: Dolly Parton*. London: Omnibus, 2007.

Morales, Helen. *Pilgrimage to Dollywood: A Country Music Road Trip through Tennessee*. Chicago: University of Chicago Press, 2014.

Munro, Michael. "Dollywood or Bust." *60 Minutes* (Australia). 9Now. June 1986.

Myers, Bonnie Trentham. *The Walker Sisters: Sprited Women of the Smokies*. Maryville, TN: Myers and Myers, 2004.

Nash, Alanna. *Dolly*. Los Angeles: Reed, 1978.

Parton, Dolly. *Dolly: My Life and Other Unfinished Business*. New York: HarperCollins, 1994.

———. *Dream More*. New York: Putnam, 2012.

———. Interview by Nate Berkus. *The Nate Berkus Show*. September 15, 2010. Distributed by Sony Pictures Television, Culver City, CA.

Parton, Willadeene. *In the Shadow of a Song*. New York: Bantam, 1985.

———. *Smoky Mountain Memories*. Nashville: Rutledge Hill, 1996.

Penman, Susie. "Cracker Barrel's Culture: Exporting the South on America's Interstate Exits." Master's thesis, University of Mississippi, 2012.

Peterson, Richard A. *Creating Country Music: Fabricating Authenticity*. Chicago: University of Chicago Press, 1997.

Petrusich, Amanda. *It Still Moves: Lost Songs, Lost Highways, and the Search for the Next American Music*. New York: Faber and Faber, 2008.

Pruitt, Cenate. "Stand by Your Man, Redneck Woman: Towards a Historical View of Country Music Gender Roles." Master's thesis, Georgia State University, 2006.

Roberts, Mark Allen. "Hillbilly Authentication: Investigating Authentic Regional Identity in Postmodern Appalachian Culture." Master's thesis, Union Institute and University, Cincinnati, 2007.

Schaffer, Gavin. "'Scientific' Racism Again?" *Journal of American Studies* (2007) 41: 253–78.

Shapiro, Henry D. *Appalachia on Our Mind: The Southern Mountains and Mountaineers in the American Consciousness, 1870–1920.* Chapel Hill: University of North Carolina Press, 1978.

Shusterman, Richard. "Moving Truth: Affect and Authenticity in Country Musicals." *Journal of Aesthetics and Art Criticism* 57, no. 2 (Spring 1999): 221–33.

Skelly, Joe. Personal communication. Email. August 27, 2014.

Smith, Richard. *Can't You Hear Me Callin': The Life of Bill Monroe, Father of Bluegrass.* Boston: Da Capo, 2000.

Sontag, Susan. "Notes on Camp." 1964. http://faculty.georgetown.edu/irvinem/theory/Sontag-NotesOnCamp-1964.html.

Sorkin, Michael. *Variations on a Theme Park: Scenes from the New American City and the End of Public Space.* New York: Hill and Wang, 1992.

Stanonis, Anthony J., ed. *Dixie Emporium: Tourism, Foodways, and Consumer Culture in the American South.* Athens: University of Georgia Press, 2008.

Starnes, Richard D. *Creating the Land of the Sky: Tourism and Society in Western North Carolina.* Tuscaloosa: University of Alabama Press, 2005.

———. "Tourism, Landscape, and History in the Great Smoky Mountains National Park." In *Destination Dixie: Tourism and Southern History,* ed. Karen L. Cox, 267–84. Gainesville: University Press of Florida, 2012.

Taylor, Charles. *Modern Social Imaginaries.* Durham, NC: Duke University Press, 2004.

Thompson, John B. *Studies in the Theory of Ideology.* Berkeley: University of California Press, 1984.

Tyson, Tim. Interviewed on "Little War on the Prairie." Episode 479 of *This American Life.* National Public Radio. November 23, 2012.

Uhlmann, Tai, dir. *For the Love of Dolly.* New Almaden, CA: Wolfe Video, 2008.

Van Dommelen, David. *Allen H. Eaton: Dean of American Crafts.* Pittsburgh: Local History, 2004.

Weyl, Nathaniel. "The Geography of Stupidity in the U.S.A." *Mankind Quarterly,* October 1974.

Whisnant, Anne Mitchell. *Super-Scenic Motorway: A Blue Ridge Parkway History.* Chapel Hill: University of North Carolina Press, 2006.

Whisnant, David E. *All That Is Native & Fine: The Politics of Culture in an American Region.* Chapel Hill: University of North Carolina Press, 1983.

Wilgus, D. K. "Country-Western Music and the Urban Hillbilly." *Journal of American Folklore* 83, no. 328 (1970): 157–79.

Williams, Michael Ann. *Homeplace.* Charlottesville: University of Virginia Press, 1991.

Wray, Matt. *Not Quite White: White Trash and the Boundaries of Whiteness.* Durham, NC: Duke University Press, 2006.

Index